MW01297386

HTML

Beginner's Guide to HTML to Master your Web Designing

JOSH STEVEN

© Copyright 2019 Josh Steven - All rights reserved.

This document is geared towards providing exact and reliable information in regards to the topic and issue covered. The publication is sold with the idea that the publisher is not required to render accounting, officially permitted or otherwise qualified services. If advice is necessary, legal or professional, a practiced individual in the profession should be ordered.

- From a Declaration of Principles which was accepted and approved equally by a Committee of the American Bar Association and a Committee of Publishers and Associations.

In no way is it legal to reproduce, duplicate, or transmit any part of this document in either electronic means or printed format. Recording of this publication is strictly prohibited, and any storage of this document is not allowed unless with written permission from the publisher. All rights reserved.

The information provided herein is stated to be truthful and consistent, in that any liability, in terms of inattention or otherwise, by any usage or abuse of any policies, processes, or directions contained within is the sole and utter responsibility of the recipient reader. Under no circumstances will any legal responsibility or blame be held against the publisher for any reparation, damages, or monetary loss due to the information herein, either directly or indirectly.

Respective authors own all copyrights not held by the publisher.

The information herein is offered for informational purposes solely and is universal as so. The presentation of the information is without a contract or any guarantee assurance.

The trademarks that are used are without any consent, and the publication of the trademark is without permission or backing by the trademark owner. All trademarks and brands within this book are for clarifying purposes only and are owned by the owners themselves, not affiliated with this document.

TABLE OF CONTENTS

Preface

Before learning the HTML language, you must have the basic knowledge of working with the Windows, Linux, or Mac operating systems. Moreover, you should have the following:

- Experience of working on text editors just like notepad, or notepad ++, etc.

- Knowledge of creating directories on your computer system.

- Knowledge of navigating through particular files and directories.

- Knowledge of images in a different types of formats such as PNG, JPG, JPEG.

This book is to learn not only how to create web pages but also it assists you in saving loading, opening the pages on a browser, fixing, and updating the web pages. "Beginners guide to HTML to master your web designing" is written to dispense the complete awareness about the Hypertext Markup Language to the readers.

Chapter 1

HTML Overview

Introduction

First of all, we have to know what HTML is. **HTML** stands for Hypertext Markup Language, which is the most widely learned language for web development. Sir Tim Berners-Lee developed it in 1991. It was officially revealed in 1995 and was named HTML 2.0 version. After that, in 1999, an advanced and major version of HTML was released that was named HTML 4.0. HTML was a fast-growing language. Many computer scientists worked on it, and soon after the 2nd version, its 3rd version was released by Dave Raggett with advance features and characteristics for developers to create elegant web pages (Raggett, 1996). After 4.0, its new version 4.0.1 was launched, which was the most successful version of HTML. Currently, HTML 5.0 version is the latest version, worldwide. It is the extended form of HTML 4.0.1.

The term Hypertext describes how HTML pages are connected on the web. This connection is known as hypertext. On the other hand, the term markup defines how tags are used to structure the text into a documented web page. It also tells the browser how to structure all text into the document and display it on the screen, such as headings, paragraphs, font styles, and colors. HTML subsists of different elements that are described by tags. All web pages in HTML are designed with the help of multiple tags. (Musciano, 1996)

HTML is a set of predefined tags that are used to create web pages. These tags are interpreted by different browsers like Safari, Mozilla Firefox, Google Chrome, Internet Explorer, Microsoft Edge, and other browsing applications. The HTML content is written on different editors like Notepad, Dreamweaver, Sublime, etc. And are saved with an extension of **.htm** or **.html**.

Some features of HTML are as follows:

- HTML is easy to learn and code.

- HTML is a platform-independent language.

- We can use all types of data, such as text, audios, and videos on our web page.

- Links or hypertexts can also be used in HTML.

- It also supports other programming languages such as CSS, JavaScript, PHP, etc.

Why Should you Learn HTML?

Hypertext Markup Language is essential to learn for students and working developers to become a tremendous Software Developer, specifically when they are willing to work in Web Development. Here are some advantages of learning:

- **Web Creation**

By learning, you can create a new one or can customize an existing website accordingly to your requirements. HTML is an essential component to learn before starting web development.

- **Start a career as a Web Developer**

You can start your career as a web developer and can earn a lot of money to secure your future.

- **Ease of learning other languages**

When you learned the building blocks of HTML, then it will be much easier for you to learn other languages such as JavaScript, PHP, Nodejs, etc.

Applications of HTML are Website Development, Responsive User-Interface Design, Internet Navigation and Game Development.

Basic HTML Page Structure

Basic page structure of an HTML page in typical form is:

```
<! DOCTYPE html>     - Page definition tag
<html>          - Root tag of document
<head>          - Header tag
<title> Title Goes Here </ title>    - Title tag
</ head>
<body>     - Body tag includes content of the page
</ body>
</ html>
```

Basic HTML Tags

HTML page consists of the following element tags:

Declaration Tag

This is the starting tag of an HTML webpage that tells the browser about the version of HTML language. This tag shows that the current version of the HTML is 4.0. It is represented as **<! DOCTYPE html>**.

Example of the Declaration tag is:

```
<! DOCTYPE html>    //Here is the Declaration tag
in the html web page.
<html>
<head>
<title> </ title>
</ head>
<body>
</ body>
</ html>
```

Root Tag

It is the root tag of the HTML page. All the content of the HTML page is written between this tag. It also has a closing tag with a backslash placed at the start of the tag. These types of tags are also known as containers. It is represented as **<html>**. Example of the <html> tag is:

```
<! DOCTYPE html>
```

```
<html>        //Here is the <html> tag in the html
web page.

<head>

<title> </ title>

</head>

<body>

</ body>

</ html>
```

Header Tag

It is known as the header of the document page. It contains information about the HTML page. It contains the title tag that describes the description of your web page. It also has a closing tag after the title tag. It is represented as **<head>**. Example of the <head> tag is:

```
<! DOCTYPE html>

<html>

<head>        //Here is the <head> tag in the html
web page.

<title> </ title>

</ head>

<body>

</ body>

</ html>
```

Title Tag

The title tag is placed within the head tag of the document. It consists of the description of the page that is being viewed. It is represented as <**title**>. Example of the title tag is:

```
<! DOCTYPE html>

<html>

<head>

<title> My First page. </ title> //Here is the
<title> tag in the html web page.

</ head>

<body>

</ body>

</ html>
```

Output:

This code shows the title of the web page as My First page.

Body Tag

It contains all the content of the page that is displayed on the screen. The body of an HTML page includes texts, headings, paragraphs, pictures and all the visible components of the web page. It is represented as <**body**>. Example of the body tag is:

```
<! DOCTYPE html>

<html>

<head>

<title> My First page. </ title>
```

```
</ head>

<body>    //Here is the <body> tag in the html web
page.

</ body>

</ html>
```

Output:

Any content written in the body tag will be displayed on the screen.

Heading Tags

This tag is used to identify the headings on the screen. There are 6 types of heading tags used in HTML that are represented as **<h1>** to **<h6>**. For example:

```
<! DOCTYPE html>

<html>

<head>

<title> My First page. </ title>

</ head>

<body>

<h1> My first heading </ h1>

<h2> My second heading </ h2>

<h3> My third heading </ h3>

<h4> My fourth heading </ h4>

<h5> My fifth heading </ h5>

<h6> My sixth heading </ h6>

</ body>
```

```
</ html>
```

Output:

My first heading

My second heading

My third heading

My fourth heading

My fifth heading

My sixth heading

Paragraph Tag

This tag includes the textual content of the web page. It is used to add paragraphs in an HTML document. It is represented as **\<p\>**. Example:

```
<! DOCTYPE html>

<html>

<head>

<title> My First page. </ title>

</ head>

<body>
```

```
<p> My name is John and I'm learning the HTML. </
p>

<p> It is the second paragraph of my web page. </
p>

</ body>

</ html>
```

Output:

My name is John and I'm learning the HTML.

It is the second paragraph of my web page.

Line Break Tag

This tag is used in HTML when we want to break the existing line and wanted to shift the remaining content into the next line in the document. The break line tag does not need a closing tag. It is represented as **<br / >**. On some browsers, it produces errors in breaking lines. Then we can use **
** for a line break.

Example of using break line tag:

```
<! DOCTYPE html>

<html>

<head>

<title> My First page. </ title>

</ head>

<body>
```

```
<p> My name is John. <br / > I'm learning the
HTML. </ p>

</ body>

</ html>
```

Output:

My name is John.

I'm learning the HTML.

Content Centering Tag

This tag is used to centralize the content on the browser screen. We just have to place the content in the opening and closing center tags to place the text at the center of the page. It is represented as **<center>** content........! **</ center>**. Example:

```
<! DOCTYPE html>

<html>

<head>

<title> My First page. </ title>

</ head>

<body>

<p> This line is not in the center of web page.
</ p>

<center>

<p> This line is in the center of web page. </ p>

</ center>

</ body>
```

```
</ html>
```

Output:

This line is not in the center of web page.

This line is in the center of the web page.

Horizontal Line Tag

This tag is used to include a visual line on the webpage and breaks the document into sections. It is represented as **<hr>.** It does not need and closing tag. Example:

```
<! DOCTYPE html>
<html>
<head>
<title> My First page. </ title>
</ head>
<body>
<p> My name is John and I'm learning the HTML. </
p>
<hr>
<p> This line is after a section break. </ p>
</ body>
</ html>
```

Output:

My name is John and I'm learning the HTML.

This line is after a section break.

Preserve Formatting Tag

It is used when we wanted to display the text in the prescribed format on web page. Text enclosed in the opening and closing preserve tag is displayed exactly in the same format on the screen in which it is written in the editor. It is represented as **<pre>** text………………! **</ pre>**. Example:

```
<! DOCTYPE html>

<html>

<head>

<title> My First page. </ title>

</ head>

<body>

<pre>
```

Some-function function-name (parameter)

```
{

    Function-logic;

}

</ pre>

</ body>

</ html>
```

Output:

Some-function function-name (parameter)

```
{

    Function-logic;

}
```

Single Space Tag

This tag is used to insert a single and nonbreaking space into the text. It is used when we don't want the web browser to break the text into next line. It is represented as ** **

Example:

```
<! DOCTYPE html>
<html>
<head>
<title> My First page. </ title>
</ head>
<body>
<p>  My  name  is  John.  I'm  "learning 
the  HTML". </ p>
</ body>
</ html>
```

Output:

My name is John. I'm "learning the HTML".

Anchor Tag

Anchor tag is used to attach a hyperlink in our web page. It appears like a link on web page. When user clicks on the link it takes the visitors to the linked web page.

Example:

```
<! DOCTYPE html>
```

```
<html>

<head>

<title> My First page. </ title>

</ head>

<body>

<p> Click the link to open it. <br /> <a href =
"https: // www.google.com"> Google <a/ > </ p>

</ body>

</ html>
```

Output:

Click the link to open it.

Google

Article Tag

Article tag is used to create and post articles, posts, blogs on the web pages in HTML. A tag named as <article>is used to create the blogs.

Example:

```
<! DOCTYPE html>

<html>

<head>

<title> My First page. </ title>

</ head>

<body>
```

```
<article> <h2> Here is the Heading </ h2> Click
the link to open it. <br /> <a href = "https: //
www.google.com"> Google </a>
</ article>
</ body>
</ html>
```

Output:

Here is the Heading

Click the link to open it.

Google

Chapter 2

HTML Elements & Attributes

Elements

Everything is written or placed within the opening, and closing tags in HTML is known as an element. The elements that do not have any content are called void elements. This type of element does not need to be closed. Examples of HTML elements are as follows:

Starting Tag	Content of Element	Ending Tag
`<p>`	It is the content of the paragraph element.	`</ p>`
`<hr />`	This is the void element in HTML.	

Nested Elements

Elements within the other elements used in HTML are known nested elements. HTML allow us to use multiple nested elements in our webpage. Example of nested elements is:

```
<! DOCTYPE html>

<html>

<head>
```

```
<title> My First page. </ title>
</ head>
<body>
<p> My name is <b> < u> John. </ u> </ b> </ p>
<p> I'm learning the HTML. </ p>
</ body>
</ html>
```

Output:

My name is **John**.

I'm learning the HTML.

Attributes

Attribute in HTML are used to provide the additional information and describe the characteristics of elements. It is placed in the opening tag of an element. It consists of two things: name and value of the attribute. All HTML elements can have attributes. Attributes used in HTML are also case-sensitive. So, they should be written in lowercase letters. Example of HTML attribute is:

```
<! DOCTYPE html>
<html>
<head>
<title> My First page. </ title>
</ head>
<body>
<p align = "right"> My name is John. </ p>
```

```
<p align = "left"> I'm learning the HTML. </ p>
</ body>
</ html>
```

Output:

My name is John.

I'm learning the HTML.

Generic HTML Attributes

Some of the core and generic attributes that are mostly used in HTML elements are:

- **title Attribute**

It is used to assign a title to the element. It pops the suggested title when cursor is moved over the content of element. Syntax for title attribute is as follows:

```
<tag-name title = "suggested title"> content </
closing tag-name>
```

Example:

```
<! DOCTYPE html>
<html>
<head>
<title> My First page. </ title>
</ head>
<body>
```

```
<p title = "User's Name!" > My name is John. </
p>

</ body>

</ html>
```

Output:

My name is John.

It displays the content written in the paragraph as it is on the screen. When we move the cursor over the text, it previews the title of the element as long as the cursor stays on the text.

- **style Attribute**

It is used to include CSS (Cascade Style Sheet) in an element to change its style and appearance. Example of style attribute is:

```
<! DOCTYPE html>

<html>

<head>

<title> My First page. </ title>

</ head>

<body>

<p style = "color: #0000FF; font-family: Calibri"
> My name is John. </ p>

</ body>

</ html>
```

Output:

My name is John.

• dir Attribute

It is used to set the direction of text flow on the browser screen. dir attribute tells the browser in which direction text should flow on the screen. The dir attribute is written in the html tag. There are two options used in dir tag that are **ltr, rtl.** Example for dir attribute is:

```
<! DOCTYPE html>

<html dir ="rtl">

<head>

<title> My First page. </ title>

</ head>

<body>

<p> This line flows from right to left on the web
page. </ p>

</ body>

</ html>
```

Output:

This line flows from right to left on the web page.

• lang Attribute

It is used to define the language that is mainly used in your web page. It works only in earlier versions of HTML. Now in advanced HTML xml: lang attribute is used for specifying the language in a web document. So, now we avoid the lang attribute and learn about the xml: lang attribute. It is also placed within the html tag. Example of xml: lang is:

```
<! DOCTYPE html>

<html xml: lang ="en">

<head>

<title> My First page. </ title>

</ head>

<body>

<p> The language used in this page is English
language. </ p>

</ body>

</ html>
```

Output:

The language used in this page is English language.

Using Chinese Language in Web page:

```
<! DOCTYPE html>

<html xml: lang ="zh">

<head>

<title> My First page. </ title>

</ head>

<body>

<p> The language used in this page is Chinese
language. </ p>

</ body>

</ html>
```

Output:

The language used in this page is Chinese language.

Using Arabic Language in Web page:

```
<! DOCTYPE html>

<html xml: lang ="ar">

<head>

<title> My First page. </ title>

</ head>

<body>

<p> The language used in this page is Arabic
language. </ p>

</ body>

</ html>
```

Output:

The language used in this page is Arabic language.

- **href attribute**

It is used to add a specific link to a location or other web page on the content of the page. When the user clicks on the text or picture that have href attribute control switches to the address mentioned in the href attribute. It is written in <a> tag. Example of href attribute is:

```
<! DOCTYPE html>

<html>

<head>
```

```
<title> My First page. </ title>

</ head>

<body>

<p> My name is John. </ p>

<a href = " www.google.com"> Here is the link.
</a>

</ body>

</ html>
```

Output:

My name is John.

Here is the link.

List of Generic Attributes

Here are the names and functionality of other attributes used in HTML.

Attribute Name	Associated Tag	Functionality
Align	<p>, <h>, <a>, <img>	Aligns the text according to the position specified.
Action	<form>	Defines the destination location to send a form of data when it is submitted.
Accept	<input>	Defines the types of files that are accepted by the server.

Alt	\<img\>, \<area\>, \<input\>	Defines the alternative textual message when a file or image can't be accessed or loaded.
Async	\<script\>	It is used for the external scripts to identify that the script is executed.
Autoplay	\<video\>, \<audio\>	It indicates that the video or audio will automatically be played when the page loads.
Autocomplete	\<input\>, \<form\>	It defines whether the autocomplete option on input or form is enabled or not.
Bgcolor	\<html\>, \<body\>, \<div\>	If is used to add a background color at any part of the web page.
Cite	\<q\>, \<ins\>, \<del\>, \<blockquote\>	It is used to allocate a specific URL which further explain the quoted, deleted or inserted text.
Class	Universal Attribute	It is used to define the class name for an element on the web page.
Contenteditable	Universal Attribute	It describes whether

		the content of an element on the web page is editable or not.
Datetime	<ins>, <time>, <ins>	It is used to define the date and time in an element.
Download	<area>, <a>	It is used to download the target file when the user clicks on a link.
Draggable	Universal Attribute	It is used to define whether an element on a web page can be dragged or not.
Height	<embed>, <iframe>, <canvas>, <img>, <video>, <object>, <input>	It is used to define the height of an element on a web page.
Multiple	<select>, <input>	It is used to define that the user can input multiple values.
Name	<select>, <button>, <object>, <form>, < textarea>, <param>, <meta>, <fieldset>, <map>, <output>, <input>, <iframe>	It is used to define the name of an element used in the web page.
Onclick	All visual objects or elements	It executes a predefined script when the user clicks the specific element.
Onchange	All visual objects or	It executes a

	elements	predefined script when the value of an element is changed.
Onerror	<img>, <object>, <audio>, <video>, <body>, <style>, <embed>, <script>	It executes a predefined script when an error is occurred on web page.
Translate	Universal Attribute	It is used to describe whether the content on the page has to be translated or not.
Wrap	<textarea>	It is used to wrap the text in text area.

Chapter 3

HTML Text Formatting

Text Formatting

Text formatting refers to changing or modifying the shape and appearance of the text on the web page. HTML allows different types of text formatting using multiple tags that are available. This feature is used to make the text visually more attractive and to present it in the prescribed form. Ten types of formatting allowed in the HTML and XHTML are defined one by one.

Bold Text Tag

It is used to bold the desired text on the browser screen. Text that is required to make bold is written as:

<b> Place content here…..! </ b>

Example:

```
<! DOCTYPE html>

<html>

<head>

<title> My First page. </ title>

</ head>

<body>

<p> It is the example of simple text. </ p>
```

```
<p> <b> It is the example of bold text. </ b> </
p>
</ body>
</ html>
```

Output:

It is an example of a simple text.

It is the example of bold text.

Italic Text Tag

It is used to italicize the desired text on the browser screen. Text that is required to make italic is written as:

<i> Place content here…..! </ i>

Example:

```
<! DOCTYPE html>
<html>
<head>
<title> My First page. </ title>
</ head>
<body>
<p> It is the example of simple text. </ p>
<p> <i> It is the example of italic text. </ i>
</ p>
</ body>
```

```
</ html>
```

Output:

It is the example of simple text.

It is the example of italic text.

Underline Text Tag

It is used to underline the desired text on the browser screen. Text that is required to make underlined is written as: **<u> Place content here.....! </ u>**

Example:

```
<! DOCTYPE html>
<html>
<head>
<title> My First page. </ title>
</ head>
<body>
<p> It is the example of simple text. </ p>
<p> <u> It is the example of italic text. </ u>
</ p>
</ body>
</ html>
```

Output:

It is the example of simple text.

It is an example of underlined text.

Strike Text Tag

It is used to strikethrough the desired text on the browser screen. A thin line bar is placed on the text that I written in the strikethrough tag. It is written as: **<strike> Place content here…..! </ strike>**

Example:

```
<! DOCTYPE html>

<html>

<head>

<title> My First page. </ title>

</ head>

<body>

<p> It is the example of simple text. </ p>

<p> It is the example of <strike> Strikethrough
</ strike> text. </ p>

</ body>

</ html>
```

Output:

It is the example of simple text.

It is the example of ~~Strikethrough~~ text.

31

Monospaced Text Tag

As we know that different alphabets take different width on the screen. By using monospaced tag each letter written in this tag will take equal space on the browser screen. It is written as: **<monospaced> Place content here…..! </ monospaced>**

Example:

```
<! DOCTYPE html>

<html>

<head>

<title> My First page. </ title>

</ head>

<body>

<p> It is the example of simple text. </ p>

<p> It is the example of <monospaced> monospaced
</ monospaced> text. </ p>

</ body>

</ html>
```

Output:

It is the example of simple text.

It is an example of monospaced text.

Superscript Text Tag

It is used to display the desired text half character above from the other characters. It is written as: **^{Place content here…..!}**

Example:

```
<! DOCTYPE html>
<html>
<head>
<title> My First page. </ title>
</ head>
<body>
<p> It is the example of simple text. </ p>
<p> It is the example of <sup> superscript </ sup> text. </ p>
</ body>
</ html>
```

Output:

It is the example of simple text.

It is an example of ^{superscript} text.

Subscript Text Tag

It is used to display the desired text half character down from the other characters. It is written as: **<sub> Place content here…..! </ sub>**

Example:

```
<! DOCTYPE html>
<html>
<head>
<title> My First page. </ title>
</ head>
<body>
<p> It is the example of simple text. </ p>
<p> It is the example of <sub> subscript </ sub>
text. </ p>
</ body>
</ html>
```

Output:

It is an example of simple text.

It is an example of subscript text.

Insert Text Tag

It is used to insert the desired text in the web page. It puts the desired content in underlined form anywhere the <ins> tag is written. It is written as: **<ins> Place content here.....! </ ins>**

Example:

```
<! DOCTYPE html>
<html>
<head>
<title> My First page. </ title>
</ head>
<body>
<p> It is the example of simple text. </ p>
<p> It is the example of <ins> inserted </ ins>
text. </ p>
</ body>
</ html>
```

Output:

It is the example of simple text.

It is an example of <u>inserted</u> text.

Delete Text Tag

It is used to put a cutting line on the desired text and to put new text instead of the existing text. It is written as: **<del> Place content here.....! </ del>**

Example:

```
<! DOCTYPE html>

<html>

<head>

<title> My First page. </ title>

</ head>

<body>

<p> It is the example of simple text. </ p>

<p> It is the example of <del> deleted </ del>
<ins> inserted </ ins> text. </ p>

</ body>

</ html>
```

Output:

It is the example of simple text.

It is the example of deleted inserted text.

Bigger Text Tag

It is used to increase the size of selected text as compared to the rest of the text. It is written as: **<big> Place content here…..! </ big>**

Example:

```
<! DOCTYPE html>

<html>

<head>

<title> My First page. </ title>

</ head>

<body>

<p> It is the example of simple text. </ p>

<p> It is the example of  <big> Bigger </ big>
text. </ p>

</ body>

</ html>
```

Output:

It is the example of simple text.

It is the example of Bigger text.

Smaller Text Tag

It is used to reduce the size of selected text as compared to the rest of the text. It is written as: **<small> Place content here…..! </ small>**

Example:

```
<! DOCTYPE html>
<html>
<head>
<title> My First page. </ title>
</ head>
<body>
<p> It is the example of simple text. </ p>
<p> It is the example of <small> Smaller </ small> text. </ p>
</ body>
</ html>
```

Output:

It is the example of simple text.

It is the example of Smaller text.

Grouped Text Tag

It is used to group different elements to created divisions or sections of a web page. It is written as: **<div> Place content here…..! </ div>**

Example:

```
<! DOCTYPE html>
<html>
<head>
<title> My First page. </ title>
</ head>
<body>
<div id =" first" align =" left" >
<h1> It is the First Heading. </ h1>
<p> It is the first paragraph. </ p>
</ div>
<div id =" second" align =" right" >
<h2> It is the Second Heading. </ h2>
<p> It is the second paragraph. </ p>
</ div>
<div id =" third" align =" right" >
<h3> It is the Third Heading. </ h3>
<p> It is the third paragraph. </ p>
</ div>
<div id =" forth" align =" right" >
```

```
<h4> It is the Fourth Heading. </ h4>

<p> It is the fourth paragraph. </ p>

</ div>

<div id =" fifth" align =" right" >

<h5> It is the Fifth Heading. </ h5>

<p> It is the fifth paragraph. </ p>

</ div>

<div id =" sixth" align =" right" >

<h6> It is the Sixth Heading. </ h6>

<p> It is the sixth paragraph. </ p>

</ div>

</ body>

</ html>
```

Output:

It is the First Heading.

It is the first paragraph.

It is the Second Heading.

It is the second paragraph.

It is the Third Heading.

It is the third paragraph.

It is the Fourth Heading.

It is the fourth paragraph.

It is the Fifth Heading.

It is the fifth paragraph.

It is the Sixth Heading.

It is the sixth paragraph.

Chapter 4

HTML Phrase Tags

Phrase Tags

These tags are used for special purposes, and they produce results, just like the formatting tags. But phrase tags include some special tags that have specific functionality. Types and explanation of phrase tags are:

Emphasize Text Tag

It is used to emphasize the desired text on the web page. It is written in the opening and closing tags such as: **<em> Place text here…..1 </ em>**.

Example:

```
<! DOCTYPE html>

<html>

<head>

<title> My First page. </ title>

</ head>

<body>

<p> It is the example of simple text. </ p>
```

```
<p> <em> It is the example of emphasized text. </
em> </p>

</ body>

</ html>
```

Output:

It is the example of simple text.

It is an example of emphasized text.

Marked Text Tag

It is used to mark the desired text with yellow color on the web page. It is written in the opening, and closing tags such as: **<mark> Place text here…..1 </ mark>**.

Example:

```
<! DOCTYPE html>

<html>

<head>

<title> My First page. </ title>

</ head>

<body>

<p> It is the example of simple text. </ p>

<p> <mark> It is the example of Marked text. </
mark> </ p>

</ body>
```

```
</ html>
```

Output:

It is the example of simple text.

It is the example of Marked text.

Strong Text Tag

It is used to display the desired text as an important text on the web page. Strong text looks bold and shiny when it appears on the screen. It is written in the opening and closing tags such as: **<strong> Place text here.....1 </ strong>**.

Example:

```
<! DOCTYPE html>

<html>

<head>

<title> My First page. </ title>

</ head>

<body>

<p> It is the example of simple text. </ p>

<p> It is the example of <strong> Strong </
strong> text. </ p>

</ body>

</ html>
```

Output:

It is the example of simple text.

It is the example of **Strong** text.

Text Abbreviation Tag

It is used to set the abbreviation of the desired text on the web page. When the cursor is moved onto the abbreviated text, it previews the abbreviation of that text, which is already mentioned in the tag. It is written in the opening and closing tags such as: **<abbr> Place text here.....1 </ abbr>**.

Example:

```
<! DOCTYPE html>

<html>

<head>

<title> Text Abbreviation </ title>

</ head>

<body>

<p> <abbr title =" Johnathon"> Jonny </ abbr> is
my best friend. </ p>

</ body>

</ html>
```

Output:

Jonny is my best friend.

Acronym Text Tag

It is used to display the desired text as the acronym text on the web page. It does not affect the original appearance of the text. It is written in the opening and closing tags such as: **<acronym> Place text here.....1 </ acronym>**.

Example:

```
<! DOCTYPE html>
<html>
<head>
<title> My First page. </ title>
</ head>
<body>
<p> It is the example of <acronym> ACRONYM </
acronym> text. </ p>
</ body>
</ html>
```

Output:

It is the example of ACRONYM text.

Text Direction Tag

It is used to for the Bi-directional movement of the desired text on the web page. The text written in the <bdo> tag will be displayed in opposite direction. It is written in the opening and closing tags such as: **<bdo dir ="rtl" > Place text here.....1 </ bdo>**.

Example:

```
<! DOCTYPE html>
<html>
<head>
<title> My First page. </ title>
</ head>
<body>
<p> It is the example of simple text. </ p>
<p> <bdo dir =" rtl" > It is the example of bi-
directional text. </ bdo> </ p>
</ body>
</ html>
```

Output:

It is the example of simple text.

. txet lanoitcerid-ib fo elpmaxe eht si tI

Special Term Tag

It is used to Indicate the desired text as a special term on the web page. It converts the selected text into italic. It is written in the opening and closing tags such as: **<dfn> Place text here.....1 </dfn>**.

Example:

```
<! DOCTYPE html>

<html>

<head>

<title> My First page. </ title>

</ head>

<body>

<p> It is the example of <dfn> special </ em>
text. </ p>

</ body>

</ html>
```

Output:

It is the example of *special* text.

Quoting Text Tag

It is used to display a block of the desired text as a quote on the web, page. It is used on large textual data. It is written in the opening and closing tags such as: **<blockquote> Place text here.....1 </ blockquote>**.

Example:

```
<! DOCTYPE html>
<html>
<head>
<title> My First page. </ title>
</ head>
<body>
<p> My name is John. It is the example of simple
text. </ p>
<blockquote> I am a software engineer. I have
expertise in web development, and game
development. It is the example of quoted text. </
blockquote>
</ body>
</ html>
```

Output:

My name is John. It is an example of a simple text.

I am a software engineer. I have expertise in web development and game development. It is the example of quoted text.

Short Text Quotations

It is used to putting a double quote around the desired text on the web page. It is written in the opening and closing tags such as: **<q> Place text here.....1 </ q>.**

Example:

```
<! DOCTYPE html>
<html>
<head>
<title> My First page. </ title>
</ head>
<body>
<p> It is the example of simple text. <q> It is
the example of Quoted text. </ q>
</ p>
</ body>
</ html>
```

Output:

It is the example of simple text. "It is the example of Quoted text."

Text Citation Tag

It is used to insert the citation into the desired text on the web page. It adds the new source place holder in the text. It is written in the opening and closing tags such as: **<cite> Place text here.....1 </cite>**.

Example:

```
<! DOCTYPE html>

<html>

<head>

<title> My First page. </ title>

</ head>

<body>

<p> It is the example of simple text. <cite> It is the example of cited text. </ cite> </ p>

</ body>

</ html>
```

Output:

It is the example of simple text. *It is the example of cited text.*

Computer Code Tag

It is used to place any type of programming code on the web page. It is written in the opening and closing tags such as: **<code> Place text here.....1 </ code>**.

Example:

```
<! DOCTYPE html>

<html>

<head>

<title> My First page. </ title>

</ head>

<body>

<p> It is the example of simple text. <code> It is the example of program code. </ code> </ p>

</ body>

</ html>
```

Output:

It is the example of simple text. It is the example of program code.

Keyboard Text Tag

It is used to get input from the user on the web page. It only takes input from the keyboard. It is written in the opening and closing tags such as: **<kbd> Place text here…..1 </ kbd>**.

Example:

```
<! DOCTYPE html>
<html>
<head>
<title> My First page. </ title>
</ head>
<body>
<p> It is the example of simple text. <kbd> Here
is the date inputted from keyboard. </ kbd> </ p>
</ body>
</ html>
```

Output:

It is the example of simple text. Here is the data inputted from the keyboard.

Programming Variable Tag

It is used to store the values of programming variables. This tag is used with the <pre> and <code> tags. It is written in the opening and closing tags such as: **<var> Place text here…..1 </ var>**.

Example:

```
<! DOCTYPE html>
<html>
<head>
<title> My First page. </ title>
</ head>
<body>
<p> It is the example of simple text. <code> It
is the example of variable tag: function-name
("<var> variable-name ") </ var> text. </ code>
</ p>
</ body>
</ html>
```

Output:

It is the example of simple text. It is the example of variable tag: **function-name ("variable-name")**.

Program Output Tag

It is used to display the output generated by a program on the web page. It is written in the opening and closing tags such as: **<samp> Place text here.....1 </ samp>**.

Example:

```
<! DOCTYPE html>
<html>
<head>
<title> My First page. </ title>
</ head>
<body>
<p> Here is the simple text. <samp> Here is the output generated by the program. </ samp> </ p>
</ body>
</ html>
```

Output:

Here is the simple text. Here is the output generated by the program.

Address Tag

It is used to contain the address of any location. It is written in the opening and closing tags such as: **<address> Place text here.....1 </address>**.

Example:

```
<! DOCTYPE html>
<html>
<head>
<title> My First page. </ title>
</ head>
<body>
<address> 25 - A, Walton Street, Cold Hills, New
York. </ address>
</ body>
</ html>
```

Output:

25 – A, Walton Street, Cold Hills, New York.

Chapter 5

HTML Meta Tags & Comments

Meta Tags

Tags used in HTML that holds a piece of additional information about the web pages are known as meta tags. It is referred to as the metadata about an HTML document or web pages such as keywords, names, expiry dates, and authors of the document. It is an example of empty elements in HTML so, all of the additional information about the HTML document is written within the tag. Meta tag is always used in the <head> </ head> tag. Syntax of writing meta tag is:

<meta name = "tag name" content =" value">

In the above syntax, the name refers to the name of a meta tag that is always user-defined. For example, Keywords, HTML document specification, page author's name, the previous modification date of HTML document, document refreshing and redirecting, etc.

Examples of meta tags are:

- **Defining keywords on HTML document**

Special keywords can be specified into the HTML document by using <meta> tag that are later used by the search engines to index your webpage on the first pages of google. Example:

```
<! DOCTYPE html>

<html>

<head>

<title> My First page. </ title>

<meta name = "keywords" content = "my page, HTML,
Metadata" />

</ head>

<body>

<p> Welcome to my webpage! </ p>

</ body>

</ html>
```

Output:

Welcome to my webpage!

- **Description of HTML document**

Short description about the HTML document can be specified by using <meta> tag that are later used by the search engines to index your webpage on the first pages of google. Example:

```
<! DOCTYPE html>

<html>

<head>

<title> My First page. </ title>

<meta name = "keywords" content = "my page, HTML,
Metadata" />

<meta name = "description" content = "description
about HTML page" />
```

```
</ head>
<body>
<p> Welcome to my webpage! </ p>
</ body>
</ html>
```

Output:

Welcome to my webpage!

- **Revision date of HTML document**

Revision date of the HTML document can be specified by using <meta> tag. It is used to tell the browser when will the document was updated last time. Example:

```
<! DOCTYPE html>
<html>
<head>
<title> My First page. </ title>
<meta name = "keywords" content = "my page, HTML,
Metadata" />
<meta name = "description" content = "description
about HTML page" />
<meta name = "revised" content = "webpage title,
9 / 11 / 2019" />
</ head>
<body>
<p> Welcome to my webpage! </ p>
</ body>
```

```
</ html>
```

Output:

Welcome to my webpage!

- **The automatic refreshing time of HTML document**

Refreshing time of the HTML document can be specified by using <meta> tag. It is used to automatically refresh the web page after a specific time. Example:

```
<! DOCTYPE html>

<html>

<head>

<title> My First page. </ title>

<meta name = "keywords" content = "my page, HTML,
Metadata" />

<meta name = "description" content = "description
about HTML page" />

<meta name = "revised" content = "webpage title,
9 / 11 / 2019" />

<meta http-equiv = "refresh" content = "10" />

</ head>

<body>

<p> Welcome to my webpage! </p>

</ body>

</ html>
```

Output:

Welcome to my webpage!

• Redirection of the HTML document

Redirection of the HTML document can be specified by using <meta> tag. It is used to redirect your web page to the server after a specific time. Example:

```
<! DOCTYPE html>

<html>

<head>

<title> My First page. </ title>

<meta name = "keywords" content = "my page, HTML,
Metadata" />

<meta name = "description" content = "description
about HTML page" />

<meta name = "revised" content = "webpage title,
9 / 11 / 2019" />

<meta http-equiv = "refresh" content = "10; url
=" http: // www. Mywebpage.com"" />

</ head>

<body>

<p> Welcome to my webpage! </ p>

</ body>

</ html>
```

Output:

Welcome to my webpage!

- **Cookies setting of HTML document**

Cookies the HTML document can be specified by using <meta> tag. Cookies referred to the data, saved into the text files on your computer system, used for the transfer of the information between the web browser and the web server to run you web application efficiently. Example:

```
<! DOCTYPE html>

<html>

<head>

<title> My First page. </ title>

<meta name = "keywords" content = "my page, HTML, Metadata" />

<meta name = "description" content = "description about HTML page" />

<meta name = "revised" content = "webpage title, 9 / 11 / 2019" />

<meta http-equiv = "refresh" content = "10; url = " http: // www. Mywebpage.com"" />

<meta http-equiv = "cookie" content = "login_id = abc; expires = Sunday, 10-nov-19 18:59 IST;"
/>

</ head>

<body>

<p> Welcome to my webpage! </ p>

</ body>

</ html>
```

Output:

Welcome to my webpage!

- **Defining the author's name of HTML document**

Author name of the HTML document can be specified by using <meta> tag. Example:

```
<! DOCTYPE html>

<html>

<head>

<title> My First page. </ title>

<meta name = "keywords" content = "my page, HTML,
Metadata" />

<meta name = "description" content = "description
about HTML page" />

<meta name = "author" content = "John Doe" />

</ head>

<body>

<p> Welcome to my webpage! </ p>

</ body>

</ html>
```

Output:

Welcome to my webpage!

- **Specifying character set on HTML document**

It is used to set the encoding type of the HTML web pages. Generally, web browsers use Latin1 encoding scheme to display the web pages. Example:

```
<! DOCTYPE html>

<html>

<head>

<title> My First page. </ title>

<meta name = "keywords" content = "my page, HTML, Metadata" />

<meta name = "description" content = "description about HTML page" />

<meta name = "revised" content = "webpage title, 9 / 11 / 2019" />

<meta http-equiv = "content-type" content = "charset = UTF-8; text/html" />

</ head>

<body>

<p> Welcome to my webpage! </ p>

</ body>

</ html>
```

Output:

Welcome to my webpage!

HTML Comments

A piece of code that is used in a HTML code to determine the portion of code in a complex document. Comments are neglected by the browser and help the viewer to understand the code. In HTML document comments are enclosed is <! -- ……. --> tags. Different types of comments used in HTML are as follows:

- **Single line HTML comments**

Single line comments are written only in a single line of the HTML document. It is written in the opening and closing special tag. Example:

```
<! DOCTYPE html>

<html>

<head>

<title> Example of single line comments. </title>

</ head>

<body>

<!-- It is the example of single line comment used in HTML. -->

<p> Welcome to my webpage! </ p>

</ body>

</ html>
```

Output:

Welcome to my webpage!

- **Multiline HTML comments**

Multiline comments are written in more than one line of the HTML document. It is written in multiple lines and enclosed within the opening and closing special tag. Example:

```
<! DOCTYPE html>
<html>
<head>
<title> Example of multiline comments. </ title>
</ head>
<body>
<!--
It is the example of multiline comment used in HTML.
Multiline comment consists of more than 1 line.
Here the body of HTML document starts.
-->
<p> Welcome to my webpage! </ p>
</ body>
</ html>
```

Output:

Welcome to my webpage!

• Conditional HTML Comments

Conditional comments are used to provide conditional instructions to the web browser being used. Conditional comments are only supported by the windows and can be executed in Internet Explorer. Other browsers will neglect the conditional comments. Example:

```
<! DOCTYPE html>

<html>

<head>

<title> Example of conditional comments. </title>

</ head>

<body>

<!-- [if IE 5] >

The special instructions that have to be provided to the browser will be placed here.

<! [endif] -->

<p> Welcome to my webpage! </ p>

</ body>

</ html>
```

Output:

Welcome to my webpage!

- **HTML comments using comment tags**

A pre-defined tag named as "comment tag" is also used to provide comments in the HTML document. It is supported by few internet browsers like Internet Explorer. It is not supported by the HTML5 version. Example:

```
<! DOCTYPE html>
<html>
<head>
<title> Example of using comment tag. </ title>
</ head>
<body>
<p> Welcome to my webpage! <comment> I'm learning
HTML. </ comment> I want to be a web
developer. </ p>
</ body>
</ html>
```

Output:

On Internet Explorer:

Welcome to my webpage! I want to be a web developer.

Other Browsers:

Welcome to my webpage! I'm learning HTML. I want to be a web developer.

- **Script code HTML comments**

It is used when we are using JavaScript coding along with the HTML. User must have to place the comments inside the script tag to make the internet browser work properly. Example:

```
<! DOCTYPE html>
<html>
<head>
<title> Example of scripting code comments. </title>
< script >
<!--
function.name (" I love programming. ")
// -->
< /script >
</ head>
<body>
<p> Welcome to my webpage! </ p>
</ body>
</ html>
```

Output:

I love programming.

Welcome to my webpage!

- **Style sheets HTML comments**

It is used when we are using CSS (Cascade Styling Sheet) coding along with the HTML. It is used to add styling and to improve appearance of the web page. User must have to place the comments inside the script tag to make the internet browser work properly. Example:

```
<! DOCTYPE html>
<html>
<head>
<title> Example of style sheet HTML comments. </title>
< style >
<!--
.name {
 font-color: #0000ff
// -->
</ style >
</ head>
<body>
<p> Welcome to my webpage! </ p>
</ body>
</ html>
```

Output:

Welcome to my webpage!

Chapter 6

HTML Images

Introduction

Images can also be used in the HTML web pages. Images help to understand the content or the concept of the HTML documents. Moreover, images are included to make the web pages more attractive and beautiful. Different steps to add and optimize images in the HTML documents are described below.

Inserting an Image

To add an image on your web page, we use an empty tag named as an image tag. It is denoted as **<img>.** It does not have a closing tag, and the attributes of the tag are written within the empty tag. Syntax of the image tag is:

<img src = "image source / URL" ……. Image attributes list />

Here image src refers to the path or location where the image is stored in the memory or at any server. Attributes list refers to associated attributes of the image that defines the width, length, image location, dimensions, etc.

Example of inserting an image into HTML document is:

```
<! DOCTYPE html>
```

```
<html>

<head>

<title> Example of inserting image to web page.
</ title>

</ head>

<body>

<p> Welcome to my webpage! </ p>

<img src = "/html /photo.png" alt = "Example
Image." />

</ body>

</ html>
```

Output:

Welcome to my webpage!

Setting Image Path

In our web directory, all the assets and images are placed in a specific directory and the path or location or that directory is written in the image source. Image tags must have an accurate directory path, file & folder name, and file extension.

Example of setting image path or location in HTML is:

```
<! DOCTYPE html>

<html>

<head>

<title> Example of setting image path or location
in the web page. </ title>

</ head>

<body>

<p> Welcome to my webpage! </ p>

<img src = "/html /assets /images /photo.png" alt
= "Example Image." />

</ body>

</ html>
```

Output:

Welcome to my webpage!

Setting Image Height & Width

We can set the height and width of the image accordingly to the requirements. It can be done by height and width HTML attributes. The height and width of the images can be described in terms of the percentage of the pixels.

Example of setting image height & width in HTML is:

```
<! DOCTYPE html>

<html>

<head>

<title> Example of setting height & width of an
image. </ title>

</ head>

<body>

<p> Welcome to my webpage! </ p>

<img src = "/html /assets /images /photo.png" alt
= "Example Image." height = "200" width = "250"
/>

</ body>

</ html>
```

Output:

Welcome to my webpage!

Setting Border of an Image

When we insert an image into our web page it will by default have a border around it. The thickness of the border can be increased or decreased by defining the border attribute.

Example of setting border to an image in HTML is:

```
<! DOCTYPE html>

<html>

<head>

<title> Example of setting an image border. </
title>

</ head>

<body>

<p> Welcome to my webpage! </ p>

<img src = "/html /assets /images /photo.png" alt
= "Example Image." Border = "5"/>

</ body>

</ html>
```

Output:

Welcome to my webpage!

Image Alignment in HTML

When we add an image in our HTML document by default it appears left-aligned on the screen. We can also adjust the alignment of the images on the web page by using the align attribute.

Example of aligning the position of an image in HTML is:

<! DOCTYPE html>

<html>

<head>

<title> Example of image alignment. </ title>

</ head>

<body>

<p> Welcome to my webpage! </ p>

<img src = "/html /assets /images /photo.png" alt = "Example Image." Align = "center" />

</ body>

</ html>

Output:

Welcome to my webpage!

Chapter 7

HTML Tables

The collection of rows and columns are known as tables. In HTML web pages tables are used to present data in the form of tables. Different operations that can be performed on HTML tables are defined below.

Creating HTML Table

In HTML, tables can be added to our web page by using the table tag. All the attributes and entities of the table are enclosed in the opening and closing table tags. The syntax for creating a table is:

```
<table>
<tr>
<td>
</ td>
</ tr>
</ table>
```

Here table tag has two main entities "**tr**" & "**td,**" tr represents the rows of the table and td represents the table data that is displayed in the table cells.

Example of adding a table into HTML document is:

```
<! DOCTYPE html>
<html>
<head>
<title> Example of adding a table. </ title>
</ head>
<body>
<p> Welcome to my webpage! </ p>
<table>
<tr>
<td> HTML </ td>
<td> CSS </ td>
<td> JavaScript </ td>
</ tr>
</ table>
</ body>
</ html>
```

Output:

Welcome to my webpage!

HTML	CSS	JavaScript

Adding Table Heading

We can also add the headings to all of the table rows. Headings are added by using **<th>** tag and replaced with the <td> tag. All the headings will be bold, and center aligned in the cells by default. Example for adding headings into HTML table is:

```html
<! DOCTYPE html>

<html>

<head>

<title> Example of adding headings on a table. </title>

</ head>

<body>

<p> Welcome to my webpage! </ p>

<table>

<tr>

<th> Course Id </ th>

<th> Course Name </ th>

<th> Instructor </ th>

</ tr>

<tr>

<td> 1 </ td>

<td> HTML </ td>

<td> Smith </ td>

</ tr>

<tr>
```

```
<td> 2 </ td>

<td> CSS </ td>

<td> Henry </ td>

</ tr>

<tr>

<td> 3 </ td>

<td> JavaScript </ td>

<td> John </ td>

</ tr>

</ table>

</ body>

</ html>
```

Output:

Welcome to my webpage!

Course Id	Course Name	Instructor
1	HTML	Smith
2	CSS	Henry
3	JavaScript	John

Manage Cell spacing and Cellpadding

We can also manage the cell spacing and cell padding of a table in HTML. Cell spacing and cellpadding refer to the white space between the cells of the table.

Example of managing cell spacing and cellpadding of a table into HTML document is:

```
<! DOCTYPE html>

<html>

<head>

<title> Example of managing cell spacing and
cellpadding in a table. </ title>

</ head>

<body>

<p> Welcome to my webpage! </ p>

<table cellspacing = "3" cellpadding = "3">

<tr>

<th> Course Id </ th>

<th> Course Name </ th>

<th> Instructor </ th>

</ tr>

<t.r>

<td> 1 </ td>

<td> HTML </ td>

<td> Smith </ td>
```

```
</ tr>

<tr>

<td> 2 </ td>

<td> CSS </ td>

<td> Henry </ td>

</ tr>

<tr>

<td> 3 </ td>

<td> JavaScript </ td>

<td> John </ td>

</ tr>

</ table>

</ body>

</ html>
```

Output:

Welcome to my webpage!

Course Id	Course Name	Instructor
1	HTML	Smith
2	CSS	Henry
3	JavaScript	John

Rows & Columns Spanning

We can also merge row or more rows or columns in a table by using "rowspan" or colspan" attributes. These attributes are placed within <td> tag to span rows or columns in HTML.

Example of rows & columns spanning of a table into HTML document is:

```
<! DOCTYPE html>

<html>

<head>

<title> Example of managing cell spacing and cellpadding in a table. </ title>

</ head>

<body>

<p> Welcome to my webpage! </ p>

<table cellspacing = "3" cellpadding = "3">

<tr>

<th> Course Id </ th>

<th> Course Name </ th>

<th> Instructor </ th>

</ tr>

<tr>

<td> 1 </ td>

<td> HTML </ td>

<td> Smith </ td>
```

```
</ tr>

<tr>

<td> 2 </ td>

<td> CSS </ td>

<td> Henry </ td>

</ tr>

<tr>

<td> 3 </ td>

<td> JavaScript </ td>

<td> John </ td>

</ tr>

</ table>

</ body>

</ html>
```

Output:

Welcome to my webpage!

Course Id	Course Name	Instructor
1	HTML	Smith
2	CSS	Henry
3	JavaScript	John

Adding Table Heading

We can also add the headings to all of the table rows. Headings are added by using **<th>** tag and replaced with the <td> tag. All the headings will be bold, and center aligned in the cells by default. Example for adding headings into HTML table is:

Example of spanning rows and columns in a table into HTML document is:

```
<! DOCTYPE html>
<html>
<head>
<title> Example of spanning in a table. </ title>
</ head>
<body>
<p> Welcome to my webpage! </ p>
<table>
<tr>
<th> Course Id </ th>
<th> Course Name </ th>
<th> Instructor </ th>
</ tr>
<tr>
<td> 1 </ td>
<td> HTML </ td>
<td> Smith </ td>
```

```
</ tr>

<tr>

<td rowspan = "3" > 2 </ td>

<td> CSS </ td>

<td> Henry </ td>

</ tr>

<tr>

<td> 3 </ td>

<td> JavaScript </ td>

<td> John </ td>

</ tr>

</ table>

</ body>

</ html>
```

Output:

Welcome to my webpage!

Course Id	Course Name	Instructor
	HTML	Smith
1 2	CSS	Henry
3	JavaScript	John

Adding Table Background

We can also add a background picture or color in a table. The "bgcolor" attribute is used to add background color in the table, and the "background" attribute is used to add a background picture in the table.

Example of adding a background of a table in HTML document is:

```
<! DOCTYPE html>

<html>

<head>

<title> Example of adding background color on a
table. </ title>

</ head>

<body>

<p> Welcome to my webpage! </ p>

<table bgcolor = "blue" >

<tr>

<th> Course Id </ th>

<th> Course Name </ th>

<th> Instructor </ th>

</ tr>

<tr>

<td> 1 </ td>

<td> HTML </ td>

<td> Smith </ td>
```

```
</ tr>

<tr>

<td> 2 </ td>

<td> CSS </ td>

<td> Henry </ td>

</ tr>

<tr>

<td> 3 </ td>

<td> JavaScript </ td>

<td> John </ td>

</ tr>

</ table>

</ body>

</ html>
```

Output:

Welcome to my webpage!

Course Id	Course Name	Instructor
1	HTML	Smith
2	CSS	Henry
3	JavaScript	John

Example of adding a background picture of a table in HTML document is:

```
<! DOCTYPE html>

<html>

<head>

<title> Example of adding background picture on a table. </ title>

</ head>

<body>

<p> Welcome to my webpage! </ p>

<table background = "/images /picture.jpg" >

<tr>

<th> Course Id </ th>

<th> Course Name </ th>

<th> Instructor </ th>

</ tr>

<tr>

<td> 1 </ td>

<td> HTML </ td>

<td> Smith </ td>

</ tr>

<tr>

<td> 2 </ td>

<td> CSS </ td>
```

```
<td> Henry </ td>

</ tr>

<tr>

<td> 3 </ td>

<td> JavaScript </ td>

<td> John </ td>

</ tr>

</ table>

</ body>

</ html>
```

Output:

Welcome to my webpage!

Course Id	Course Name	Instructor
1	HTML	Smith
2	CSS	Henry
3	JavaScript	John

Adding Table Caption

We can also add a caption to our table in the HTML document. The caption tag is referring to the title of the table and provides an idea about the explanation of the table.

Example of adding caption on a table in HTML document is:

```
<! DOCTYPE html>

<html>

<head>

<title> Example of adding caption on a table. </title>

</ head>

<body>

<p> Welcome to my webpage! </ p>

<table>

<caption> Here is the caption of the table. </caption>

<tr>

<th> Course Id </ th>

<th> Course Name </ th>

<th> Instructor </ th>

</ tr>

<tr>

<td> 1 </ td>

<td> HTML </ td>
```

```
<td> Smith </ td>

</ tr>

<tr>

<td> 2 </ td>

<td> CSS </ td>

<td> Henry </ td>

</ tr>

<tr>

<td> 3 </ td>

<td> JavaScript </ td>

<td> John </ td>

</ tr>

</ table>

</ body>

</ html>
```

Output:

Welcome to my webpage!

Here is the caption of the table.

Course Id	Course Name	Instructor
1	HTML	Smith
2	CSS	Henry
3	JavaScript	John

Example of adding caption on a table in HTML document is:

```
<! DOCTYPE html>

<html>

<head>

<title> Example of adding caption on a table. </
title>

</ head>

<body>

<p> Welcome to my webpage! </ p>

<table>

<caption style = "color: red"> Here is the
caption of the table. </ caption>

<tr>

<th> Course Id </ th>

<th> Course Name </ th>

<th> Instructor </ th>

</ tr>

<tr>

<td> 1 </ td>

<td> HTML </ td>

<td> Smith </ td>

</ tr>

<tr>

<td> 2 </ td>
```

```
<td> CSS </ td>

<td> Henry </ td>

</ tr>

<tr>

<td> 3 </ td>

<td> JavaScript </ td>

<td> John </ td>

</ tr>

</ table>

</ body>

</ html>
```

Output:

Welcome to my webpage!

Here is the caption of the table.

Course Id	Course Name	Instructor
1	HTML	Smith
2	CSS	Henry
3	JavaScript	John

Defining Table Header, Footer & Body

We can also divide an HTML table into three parts, known as Header, Body, and Footer of the table. <thead> attribute is used to create a header in the table. <tbody> is to define the body of the HTML table. <tfoot> is used to define the footer of the HTML table.

Example for defining header, body or footer of a table in HTML document is:

```
<! DOCTYPE html>

<html>

<head>

<title> Example of defining header, footer or body of a table. </ title>

</ head>

<body>

<p> Welcome to my webpage! </ p>

<table background = "/images /picture.jpg" >

<thead>

<tr>

<td> Course Id </ td>

<td> Course Name </ td>

<td> Instructor </ td> </ tr>

</ thead>

<tbody>

<tr>

<td> 1 </ td>
```

```
<td> HTML </ td>
<td> Smith </ td>
</ tr>
<tr>
<td> 2 </ td>
<td> CSS </ td>
<td> Henry </ td>
</ tr>
<tr>
<td> 3 </ td>
<td> JavaScript </ td>
<td> John </ td>
</ tr>
</ tbody>
<tfoot>
<tr>
<td> This is the footer of the table. </ td>
</ tr>
</ tfoot>
</ table>
</ body>
</ html>
```

Output:

Course Id	Course Name	Instructor
1	HTML	Smith
2	CSS	Henry
3	JavaScript	John
This is the footer of the table.		

Chapter 8

HTML Lists & Blocks

HTML Lists

We can display the list of information on our web pages by using three different types of elements. These elements are "ul," "ol," "dl." First element "ul" is used to display an unsorted list of information on the screen. "ol" is used to display the sorted list of information in an arranged scheme on the web page. "dl" element is used to display the list of items ad they are displayed into the dictionary.

Unordered HTML Lists

It is a list of collected items that are displayed on the web page without any special order or sequence. It is displayed by using <ul> tag, and all the items in this list are displayed as bullet points.

Example for unsorted list in HTML is:

```
<! Doctype html>

<html>

<head>

<title> Example to display unsorted list. </title>

</ head>

<body>
```

```
<ul>

<li> Apple </ li>

<li> Banana </ li>

<li> Mango </ li>

<li> Orange </ li>

</ ul>

</ body>

</ html>
```

Output:

- Apple

- Banana

- Mango

- Orange

Example for unsorted list with attributes in HTML is:

```
<! Doctype html>

<html>

<head>

<title> Example to display unsorted list. </ title>

</ head>

<body>
```

100

```
<ul style = "color:blue" >

<li> Apple </ li>

<li> Banana </ li>

<li> Mango </ li>

<li> Orange </ li>

</ ul>

</ body>

</ html>
```

Output:

- Apple

- Banana

- Mango

- Orange

"Type" Attribute in Unsorted List

Type attribute is used to define the type bullet points in HTML. It uses disc as a default bullet, other available types are:

<ul type = "square">

<ul type = "disc">

<ul type = "circle">

Example for **<ul type = "square">** is:

```
<! Doctype html>

<html>

<head>

<title> Example to display unsorted list. </
title>

</ head>

<body>

<ul type = "square" >

<li> Apple </ li>

<li> Banana </ li>

<li> Mango </ li>

<li> Orange </ li>

</ ul>

</ body>

</ html>
```

Output:

- ▪ Apple

- ▪ Banana

- ▪ Mango

- ▪ Orange

Example for **<ul type = "disc">** is:

```
<! Doctype html>

<html>

<head>

<title> Example to display unsorted list. </
title>

</ head>

<body>

<ul type = "disc" >

<li> Apple </ li>

<li> Banana </ li>

<li> Mango </ li>

<li> Orange </ li>

</ ul>

</ body>

</ html>
```

Output:

- Apple

- Banana

- Mango

- Orange

Example for **<ul type = "circle">** is:

```
<! Doctype html>
<html>
<head>
<title> Example to display unsorted list. </title>
</ head>
<body>
<ul type = "circle" >
<li> Apple </ li>
<li> Banana </ li>
<li> Mango </ li>
<li> Orange </ li>
</ ul>
</ body>
</ html>
```

Output:

- o Apple

- o Banana

- o Mango

- o Orange

Example for **<ul type = "circle">** is:

```
<! Doctype html>

<html>

<head>

<title> Example to display unsorted list. </
title>

</ head>

<body>

<ul type = "circle" style = "color: blue" >

<li> Apple </ li>

<li> Banana </ li>

<li> Mango </ li>

<li> Orange </ li>

</ ul>

</ body>

</ html>
```

Output:

- o Apple

- o Banana

- o Mango

- o Orange

Ordered HTML Lists

It is a list of collected items that are displayed on the web page in a series of number instead of bullets. It is displayed by using <ol> tag and all the items in this list are displayed as numbered items list.

Example for ordered list in HTML is:

```
<! Doctype html>

<html>

<head>

<title> Example to display ordered list. </title>

</ head>

<body>

<ol>

<li> Apple </ li>

<li> Banana </ li>

<li> Mango </ li>

<li> Orange </ li>

</ ol>

</ body>

</ html>
```

Output:

1. Apple

2. Banana

3. Mango

4. Orange

"Type" Attribute in Ordered Lists

Type attribute is used to define the type of numbering in the list. It uses numbers by default, other available types are:

<ul type = "1">

<ul type = "I">

<ul type = "i">

<ul type = "A">

<ul type = "a">

Example for **<ul type = "I">** is:

```
<! Doctype html>
<html>
<head>
<title> Example  to  display  ordered  list. </
title>
</ head>
<body>
<ol type = "I">
```

```
<li> Apple </ li>
<li> Banana </ li>
<li> Mango </ li>
<li> Orange </ li>
</ ol>
</ body>
</ html>
```

Output:

   I.   Apple

  II.   Banana

 III.   Mango

 IV.   Orange

Example for **<ul type = "i">** is:

```
<! Doctype html>
<html>
<head>
<title> Example to display ordered list. </
title>
</ head>
<body>
<ol type = "i">
```

```
<li> Apple </ li>

<li> Banana </ li>

<li> Mango </ li>

<li> Orange </ li>

</ ol>

</ body>

</ html>
```

Output:

   i.   Apple

   ii.   Banana

   iii.   Mango

   iv.   Orange

Example for **<ul type = "A">** is:

```
<! Doctype html>

<html>

<head>

<title>  Example  to  display  ordered  list.  </
title>

</ head>

<body>

<ol type = "A">
```

```
<li> Apple </ li>

<li> Banana </ li>

<li> Mango </ li>

<li> Orange </ li>

</ ol>

</ body>

</ html>
```

Output:

A. Apple

B. Banana

C. Mango

D. Orange

Example for **<ul type = "a">** is:

```
<! Doctype html>

<html>

<head>

<title> Example to display ordered list. </
title>

</ head>

<body>

<ol type = "a">
```

```
<li> Apple </ li>

<li> Banana </ li>

<li> Mango </ li>

<li> Orange </ li>

</ ol>

</ body>

</ html>
```

Output:

 a) Apple

 b) Banana

 c) Mango

 d) Orange

Definition Lists in HTML

It is a list of collected items that are displayed on the web page as they are mentioned in the dictionary of encyclopedia. It is displayed by using <dl> tag and other tag enclosed in the <dl> tag is:

- <dl> Refers to the start of the definition list

- <dt> Refers to a term used in the list

- <dd> Refers to the definition of the term used in the lists

- </ dl> Refers to the end of the definition list

Example for definition list in HTML is:

```
<! Doctype html>

<html>

<head>

<title> Example  to  display  definition  list. </
title>

</ head>

<body>

<dl>

<dt> <i> <b> HTML </ b> </ i> </ dt>

<dd> The term "HTML" stands for Hyper Text Markup
Language. </ dd>

<dt> <i> <b> WWW</ b> </ i> </ dt>

<dd> The term "WWW" stands for World Wide Web. </
dd>

</ dl>

</ body>

</ html>
```

Output:

HTML

The term "HTML" stands for Hyper Text Markup Language.

WWW

The term "WWW" stands for World Wide Web.

Blocks in HTML

Blocks in HTML refers to the division or partition of the elements on the screen. All HTML elements in blocks are have a line break after them. Every block in HTML starts from a new line and different block elements used in HTML are: <p>, <ul>, <ol>, <dl>, <h1>, <h2>, <h3>, <h4>, <h5>, <h6>, <hr />, <blockquote>, <pre>, and <address>. The two main tags that are used to create block or groups other block elements are <div> and <span> tags.

HTML <div> Tag

<div> tag is the most essential tag to group block elements and other HTML elements as well as it is used to apply CSS on various groups of HTML elements. This tag is mostly used with the CSS to create the web page layout and to make the appearance more attractive and understandable.

Example of using <div> tag is:

```
<! DOCTYPE html>

<html>

<head>

<title> Example of div tag </ title>

</ head>

<body>

<!-- It represents the first block or group on
web page. -->

< div style = "font-family : Arial", "color :
blue" >
```

```html
<h2> It is the first block on HTML page. </ h2>

<p> My name is John and I'm learning Web
Development. All I have to learn is: </ p>

<ol>

<li> HTML </ li>

<li>CSS </ li>

<li> JavaScript </ li>

<li> PHP </ li>

</ ol>

</ div>

<!-- It represents the second block or group on
web page. -->

< div style = "font-family : Calibri", "color :
green" >

<h2> It is the second block on HTML page. </ h2>

<p> My name is Harry and I'm a software Engineer.
I'm working for an International company. I have
expertise in: </ p>

<ol>

<li> Web Development </ li>

<li> Game Development </ li>

<li> Desktop Development </ li>

<li> Network Troubleshooting </ li>

</ ol>

</ div>

</ body>
```

```
</ html>
```

Output:

It is the first block on HTML page.

My name is John, and I'm learning Web Development. All I have to learn is:

1. HTML

2. CSS

3. JavaScript

4. PHP

It is the second block on the HTML page.

My name is Harry, and I'm a Software Engineer. I'm working for an international company. I have expertise in:

1. Web Development

2. Game Development

3. Desktop Development

4. Network Troubleshooting

HTML <span> Tag

The <span> tag in HTML is only used with the inline elements to group them. It is also used with the CSS to produce much better results and to make the layout of the HTML document more attractive. The major difference between <div> and the <span> tag is that <span> tag is used only with inline HTML elements while <div> tag is used with the clock level HTML elements.

Example of <span> tag is:

```
<! DOCTYPE html>

<html>

<head>

<title> Example of span tag </ title>

</ head>

<body>

<p> My name is Harry and I'm a software Engineer.
<span style = "color : red" > I'm working for an
International company. </ span> I have expertise
in: </ p>

<span style = "color : blue" >

    • Web Development
    • Game Development
    • Desktop Development
    • Network Troubleshooting
</ span>

</ body>

</ html>
```

Output:

My name is Harry and I'm a software Engineer. I'm working for an International company. I have expertise in:

- Web Development

- Game Development

- Desktop Development

- Network Troubleshooting

Chapter 9

HTML Links

HTML web pages may also have links that direct you to other remote locations. The remote locations may include other webpages or remote servers. When the user clicks on the link, it directly takes him/her to the particular destination location mentioned in the link. Different forms of links used in HTML are described below.

- Text Links in HTML

- Image Links in HTML

- Email Links in HTML

Text Links in HTML

A type of HTML links that are in the form of text and directs you toward another web page or to the specific portion of the existing page. Text links in HTML are also known as Hyperlinks. Text links in HTML are used for various purposes that are:

Linking a Document to HTML page

A tag named "anchor tag" is used to add a link or document to the HTML page. It is denoted as <a>, everything enclosed in the opening <a> and closing </ a> tag is treated as a text link in the HTML document. The syntax for "anchor tag" is:

<a href = "Place URL of the document here", Link attributes, Link Target = "mention link target here" > Place Link Text Here </ a>

In the above syntax URL refers to the address of the destination location, Link target refers to the location where the new link should be opened.

Different types of target attribute used in HTML are:

• **_self**

This attribute opens the linked page or document in the same frame. Means the document associated with the hyperlink will be opened in some portion of the same web page. Example for text link using _self attribute is:

```
<! DOCTYPE html>
<html>
<head>
<title> Example of text link using _self
attribute. </ title>
</ head>
<body>
<p> It is the example of HTML Text Link. </ p>
```

```
<a href = " /web /html /product.html" target =
"_self "> Click here to open the link. </ a>
</ body>
</ html>
```

Output:

It is an example of HTML Text Link.

Click here to open the link.

- **_blank**

This attribute opens the linked page or document in the new window.
Means the document associated with the hyperlink will be opened in
the new window of the internet browser. Example for text link using
_blank attribute is:

```
<! DOCTYPE html>
<html>
<head>
<title> Example of text link using _blank
attribute. </ title>
</ head>
<body>
<p> It is the example of HTML Text Link. </ p>
<a href = " /web /html /product.html" target =
"_blank "> Click here to open the link. </ a>
</ body>
```

```
</ html>
```

Output:

It is an example of HTML Text Link.

Click here to open the link.

* **_parent**

This attribute opens the linked page or document in the parent frame. Means the document associated with the hyperlink will be opened in the parent or index page of the website. Example for text link using _parent attribute is:

```
<! DOCTYPE html>

<html>

<head>

<title> Example of text link using _parent
attribute. </ title>

</ head>

<body>

<p> It is the example of HTML Text Link. </ p>

<a href = " /web /html /product.html" target =
"_parent "> Click here to open the link. </ a>

</ body>

</ html>
```

Output:

It is an example of HTML Text Link.

Click here to open the link.

- **_top**

This attribute opens the linked page or document in the full width of the window. Means the document associated with the hyperlink will be opened in full window of the same web page. Example for text link using _top attribute is:

```
<! DOCTYPE html>
<html>
<head>
<title> Example of text link using _top attribute. </ title>
</ head>
<body>
<p> It is the example of HTML Text Link. </ p>
<a href = " /web /html /product.html" target = "_top "> Click here to open the link. </ a>
</ body>
</ html>
```

Output:

It is an example of HTML Text Link.

Click here to open the link.

- **targetframe**

This attribute opens the linked page or document in the specific frame of the named page. Means the document associated with the hyperlink will be opened in specific portion or frame of the target web page. Example for text link using _targetframe attribute is:

```
<! DOCTYPE html>
<html>
<head>
<title> Example of text link using _targetframe
attribute. </ title>
</ head>
<body>
<p> It is the example of HTML Text Link. </ p>
<a href = " /web /html /product.html" target =
"_targetframe "> Click here to open the link. </
a>
</ body>
</ html>
```

Output:

It is an example of HTML Text Link.

Click here to open the link.

Using <base> Tag

We can also add HTML text links to our web page using <base> tag. It is used when we have to add the links of the web pages or portions of the same website. For example, when we want to place a link of other web pages of the same website, we will use the <base> tag instead of the <a> tag.

```
Example for using <base> tag is:
<! DOCTYPE html>
<html>
<head>
<title> Example of text link using _self
attribute. </ title>
<base href = " https://www.mywebsite.com/ ">
</ head>
<body>
<p> It is the example of HTML Text Link. </ p>
<a href = " /web /html /product.html" target =
"_self "> Click here to open Home Page. </ a>
</ body>
</ html>
```

Output:

It is the example of HTML Text Link.

Click here to open Home Page.

Setting Colors to HTML Text Links

We can also change the color of the HTML text links by using the **link, alink**, and **vlink** attribute inside the <body> tag. Link attribute represents that the text is a link. Alink represents that is it an active link, and vlink shows that it is a visited link.

Example for using link, alink and vlink attribute is:

```
<! DOCTYPE html>

<html>

<head>

<title> Example of text link coloring attribute.
</ title>

<base href = " https://www.mywebsite.com/ ">

</ head>

<body link = " #040404 " alink = " #54A250 "
vlink = " #F00000 ">

<p> It is the example of HTML Text Link. </ p>

<a href = " /web /html /product.html" target =
"_self "> Click here to open Home Page. </ a>

</ body>

</ html>
```

Output:

It is the example of HTML Text Link.

Click here to open Home Page.

Adding Download Links

HTML also allows us to add a document downloading link on our web page. When the user clicks on the link file attached with the link will be started to be download in your system. We can attach DOC, PDF, and ZIP files in our HTML document.

Example for adding downloadable file in HTML is:

```
<! DOCTYPE html>

<html>

<head>

<title> Example of adding a file to download. </title>

</ head>

<body>

<p> It is the example of file download Link. </p>

<a href = " /web /html /product.pdf" > Click here to download the file. </ a>

</ body>

</ html>
```

Output:

It is the example of file download link.

Click here to download the file.

Image Links in HTML

HTML also allows us to create hyperlinks by using images instead of text. When the user clicks on the image, it takes the user to the particular destination location. The difference between the text link and image link is that we have to place an image in the <a> tag instead of the text.

Example for using images as hyperlink is:

```
<! DOCTYPE html>

<html>

<head>

<title> Example of Image Links in HTML </ title>

</ head>

<body>

<p> It is the example of HTML Image Link. </ p>

<a href = " /web /html /product.html" target = "_self "> <img src = "/files /assets /images /picture.png " alt = " Image Link " border = "0" > </ a>

</ body>

</ html>
```

Output:

It is the example of HTML Image Link.

Email Links in HTML

We can also attach email links to our web pages. When the user clicks on an email link it takes him to the mailbox to compose the email with the recipient email address. Using the email address in web pages causes spamming problems in the email account that is added as a recipient. It is also used to collect data from different sources such as surveys and forms.

Example for adding Email links in HTML is:

```
<! DOCTYPE html>

<html>

<head>

<title> Example of adding an email link. </title>

</ head>

<body>

<p> It is the example of HTML email Link. </ p>
```

```
<a href = " mailto:xyz@domain.com" > Click here
to send an email. </ a>
</ body>
</ html>
```

Output:

It is the example of HTML email link.

Click here to send an email.

Chapter 10

HTML Fonts

Fonts in a web page plays an essential role to make it more attractive, user-friendly and also enhance the readability. By default, font appearance fully depends upon the computer system or the internet browser that is being used. In HTML we can also set the font style, color, and size by using <font> tag. The <font> tag includes three different attributes known as size, color and face to make your content more transparent and readable. We can also use <basefont> tag to customize the whole content with as the same face, size, and color.

Setting Font Size in HTML

Font size in HTML web page can be set by using "size" attribute. The default font size in HTML is "3" but we can set it from "1 to 7". Example for setting font size is:

```
<!DOCTYPE html>
<html>
<head>
<title>Example for setting HTML Font Size</title>
</head>
<body>
<font size = "7" > I Love Programming. </ font> <br />
<font size = "6" > I Love Programming. </ font> <br />
```

```
<font size = "5" > I Love Programming. </ font> <br />

<font size = "4" > I Love Programming. </ font> <br />

<font size = "3" > I Love Programming. </ font> <br />

<font size = "2" > I Love Programming. </ font> <br />

<font size = "1" > I Love Programming. </ font>

</body>

</html>
```

Output:

I Love Programming.

I Love Programming.

I Love Programming.

I Love Programming.

I Love Programming.

I Love Programming.

I Love Programming.

Setting Font Face in HTML

Font face in HTML web page can be set by using "face" attribute. The default font size in HTML depends upon the computer or the web browser. Example for setting font face is:

```
<! DOCTYPE html>

<html>

<head>

<title> Example for setting HTML Font Face </title>

</ head>
```

```
<body>

<font size = "7" face = "Calibri" > I Love
Programming. </ font> <br />

<font size = "6" face = "Verdana" > I Love
Programming. </ font> <br />

<font size = "5" face = "Times New Roman" > I
Love Programming. </ font> <br />

<font size = "4" face = "Tempus sans ITC" > I
Love Programming. </ font> <br />

<font size = "3" face = "Bodoni MT" > I Love
Programming. </ font> <br />

<font size = "2" face = "Comic sans MS" > I Love
Programming. </ font> <br />

<font size = "1" face = "Calibri" > I Love
Programming. </ font>

</ body>

</ html>
```

Output:

I Love Programming.

I Love Programming.

I Love Programming.

I Love Programming.

I Love Programming.

I Love Programming.

I Love Programming.

Setting Font Colors in HTML

Font color in HTML web page can be set by using "color" attribute. The default font color in HTML is black. Example for setting font color is:

```
<! DOCTYPE html>

<html>

<head>

<title> Example for setting HTML Font Color </title>

</ head>

<body>

<font size = "7" color = "red" > I Love Programming. </ font> <br />

<font size = "6" color = "yellow" > I Love Programming. </ font> <br />

<font size = "5" color = "green" > I Love Programming. </ font> <br />

<font size = "4" color = "blue" > I Love Programming. </ font> <br />

<font size = "3" color = "pink" > I Love Programming. </ font> <br />

<font size = "2" color = "maroon" > I Love Programming. </ font> <br />

<font size = "1" color = "sky" > I Love Programming. </ font>

</ body>
```

```
</ html>
```

Output:

I Love Programming.

I Love Programming.

I Love Programming.

I Love Programming.

I Love Programming.

I Love Programming.

I Love Programming.

Chapter 11

HTML Colors & Backgrounds

HTML Colors

HTML allows us to set different colors to make the web page more user-friendly, attractive, and readable. Color attribute can only be defined in the <body> tag of HTML document. To set the color of the individual block or tag, we can use the bgcolor attribute. There are three different procedures to add colors to the web page:

- **Using Color Names**

It is the simplest method to add the color in your web page. User just have to write color name to add the desired color. Example for adding colors by using color name is:

```
<! DOCTYPE html>

<html>

<head>

<title> Adding colors in HTML by name. </ title>

</ head>

<body text = "red" >

<p> My name is Harry, and I'm a Software
Engineer. I'm working for an international
company. I

have expertise in:
```

```
Web Development

Game Development

Desktop Development

Network Troubleshooting

</ p>

</ body>

</ html>
```

Output:

My name is Harry, and I'm a Software Engineer. I'm working for an international company. I

have expertise in:

Web Development

Game Development

Desktop Development

Network Troubleshooting

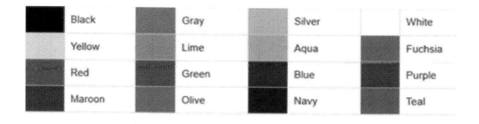

- **Using Hex Value**

It is the second method to add the color in your web page. User just have to write color Hex code to add the desired color. Example for adding colors by using Hex code is:

```
<! DOCTYPE html>

<html>

<head>

<title> Adding colors in HTML by Hex values. </
title>

</ head>

<body text = "0000FF" >

<p> My name is Harry, and I'm a Software
Engineer. I'm working for an international
company. I

have expertise in:

Web Development

Game Development

Desktop Development

Network Troubleshooting

</ p>

</ body>

</ html>
```

Output:

My name is Harry, and I'm a Software Engineer. I'm working for an international company. I

have expertise in:

Web Development

Game Development

Desktop Development

Network Troubleshooting

W3C Standard 16 Colors

Here is the list of W3C Standard 16 Colors names and it is recommended to use them.

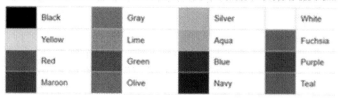

	Black		Gray		Silver		White
	Yellow		Lime		Aqua		Fuchsia
	Red		Green		Blue		Purple
	Maroon		Olive		Navy		Teal

Example

Here are the examples to set background of an HTML tag by color name –

```
<!DOCTYPE html>
<html>
```

- **Using rgb Value**

It is the third method to add the color in your web page. User just have to write color rgb scheme to add the desired color. Example for adding colors by using rgb scheme is:

```
<! DOCTYPE html>

<html>

<head>

<title> Adding colors in HTML by rgb color
scheme. </ title>

</ head>

<body text = "rgb(0, 255, 0)" >

<p> My name is Harry, and I'm a Software
Engineer. I'm working for an international
company. I

have expertise in:

Web Development

Game Development

Desktop Development

Network Troubleshooting

</ p>

</ body>

</ html>
```

Output:

My name is Harry, and I'm a Software Engineer. I'm working for an international company. I have expertise in:

Web Development

Game Development

Desktop Development

Network Troubleshooting

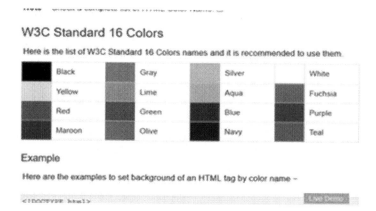

W3C Standard 16 Colors

Here is the list of W3C Standard 16 Colors names and it is recommended to use them.

	Black		Gray		Silver		White
	Yellow		Lime		Aqua		Fuchsia
	Red		Green		Blue		Purple
	Maroon		Olive		Navy		Teal

Example

Here are the examples to set background of an HTML tag by color name –

`<!DOCTYPE html>`

HTML Backgrounds

Html allows us to add background colors and images on complete web page or in a particular area. Default background color of web page is white, but we can change it by using multiple tag attributes. We have two background options in HTML that are:

Background Colors in HTML

Background colors in HTML can be changed by using "bgcolor" attribute. Syntax for changing background color in HTML is:

<tag_name bgcolor = " color_name / value " >

Example of changing background color in HTML is:

```
<! DOCTYPE html>

<html>

<head>

<title> Example of changing background color in
HTML. </ title>

</ head>

<body>

<!-- In first line we use color name in
attribute's value -->

<table bgcolor = "red" width = "50%">

<tr>

<td> This line has red color in background. </td>

</tr>

</table>


<!-- In second line we use color value in
attribute's value -->

<table bgcolor = "#4040FF" width = "50%">

<tr>
```

```
<td> This line has yellow color in background.
</td>

</tr>

</table>


<!-- In first line we use RGB color scheme in
attribute's value -->

<table bgcolor = "rgb(240, 60, 240)" width =
"50%">

<tr>

<td> This line has blue color in background.
</td>

</tr>

</table>

</body>

</html>
```

Output:

It is the example of changing background color.

This line has a red color in the background.

This line has a yellow color in the background.

This line has blue color in background

Background Images in HTML

We can also add images in the background of the entire web page, in a specific frame, in tables or in table cells. Background pictures in HTML can be changed by using "background" attribute. Syntax for setting background images in HTML is: <tag_name background = " picture / image URL " attribute list >

Example of setting background image in HTML is:

```
<! DOCTYPE html>

<html>

<head>

<title> Example of setting background image in
HTML. </ title>

</ head>

<!-- Set background image in full web page -->

<body background = " /files /assets /images
/photo.png " height = "100%" width = "100%" >

<p> My name is John. I'm a Software Engineer.
It's my first HTML web page. </ p>

</ body>

</ html>
```

Output:

The web page will display the text and a background image with full dimensions of the page.

Chapter 12

HTML Forms

Forms

Many times, we want to gather data from the users or visitors of our web pages; HTML forms are used to perform this task. When the user inputs data into the form it is stored in the database of a back-end application by scripting. Data gathered from the visitors is later used for a different type of analysis. There are multiple elements used in HTML forms to collect data that are: text fields, text area fields, checkboxes, drop-down lists, radio buttons, etc. A form in HTML is created by using <form> tag. Syntax for <form> tag is:

<form action = "URL" method = "transfer method">

Elements used in the form such as checkboxes, text area fields, drop-down lists, etc.

</form>

Different attributes used in form tag are:

- **action**

  The action attribute defines the action that has to be performed when the form is submitted.

Example for action attribute is:

```
<! DOCTYPE html>

<html>

<head>

<title> Form input element </ title>

<body>

<h4> Form input element </ h4>

<! -- Here we define the page to which the data
has to be sent -->

<form action = "/mainpahe.php" method = "POST" >

Type Name Here:

<input type = "username" type = "text" >

<br>

Type Password Here:

<input type = "userpassword" type = "password" >

<br>

<input type = "submit" >

</ form>

</ body>

</ html>
```

Output:

Form Input Element

Type Name Here: [_____]

Type Password here: [_____]

When the user clicks the submit button all the data will be forwarded
to the linked page.

- **Method**

Method attributes describe the GET or POST method while submitting the form. When we use the Get method data will be displayed in the address bar. On the other hand, when we use the POST method, the data will be transferred in encrypted form and not be displayed in the address bar.

Example for Method attribute is:

```
<! DOCTYPE html>

<html>

<head>

<title> Form input element </ title>

<body>

<h4> Form input element </ h4>

<! - all the data inputted will be sent in
encrypted for and does not show in the address
bar -->

<form action = "/mainpahe.php" method = "POST" >

Type Name Here:

<input type = "username" type = "text" >

<br>

Type Password Here:

<input type = "userpassword" type = "password" >

<br>

<input type = "submit" >

</ form>
```

```
</ body>
</ html>
```

Output:

Form Input Element

Type Name Here: [   ]

Type Password here: [   ]

When the user clicks the submit button all the data will be sent in encrypted form to the linked page.

- **Target**

The target attribute defines the target window, frame, and web page where the form has to be submitted.

- **Enctype**

Enctype attribute defines how the internet browser will encode data collected from the user before sending it to the server or destination location.

Form Elements

Different type of elements is used in HTML forms to collect input from the users or visitors. All the elements used in HTML forms are:

- **Form <input> Element**

It is an essential element of the HTML form and used to take a different type of text input from the users. It depends upon the kind of data that has to be inputted.

Example for <input> element is:

```
<! DOCTYPE html>
<html>
<head>
<title> Form input element </ title>
<body>
<h4> Form input element </ h4>
<form action = "/mainpahe.php" method = "POST" >
Type Name Here:
<input type = "username" type = "text" >
<br>
Type Password Here:
<input type = "userpassword" type = "password" >
<br>
<input type = "submit" >
</ form>
</ body>
</ html>
```

Output:

Form Input Element

Type Name Here: [   ]

Type Password here: [   ]

Submit input

Attributes of the text input are the type, value, name, size, and maxlength.

- **Form <select> Element**

It is used when multiple options are available, and the user has to select only one of them.

Example for <select> element is:

```
<! DOCTYPE html>

<html>

<head>

<title> Form select element </ title>

<body>

<h4> Select your favorite fruit from the list. </
h4>

<form action = "/mainpahe.php" method = "POST" >

<select name = "fruits" >

<option value = "apple" > Apple </ option>

<option value = "mango" > Mango </ option>

<option value = "grape" > Grape </ option>

<option value = "peach" > Peach </ option>

<option value = "banana" > Banana </ option>

<option value = "orange" > Orange </ option>

<br>

<input type = "submit" >

</ form>

</ body>

</ html>
```

Output:

Select your favorite fruit from the list.

Here the Drop-down list will appear.

Submit input

- **Form <textarea> Element**

It is used when a large size of text input is required, such as paragraphs or introduction of more than one line.

Example for <textarea> element is:

```
<! DOCTYPE html>
<html>
<head>
<title> Form textarea element </ title>
<body>
<h4> Form textarea element </ h4>
<form action = "/mainpahe.php" method = "POST" >
Type Name Here:
<textarea name = "summary" cols = "20" rows =
"20" > My name is John and I'm a software
engineer. I have expertise in C++, Web
development, Game Development, and Graphics
Designing. </ textarea>
<br>
<input type = "submit" >
```

```
</ form>

</ body>

</ html>
```

Output:

Form textarea Element

My name is John and I'm a
software engineer. I have expertise
in C++, Web development, Game
Development,   and   Graphics
Designing.

Submit input

- **Form <button> Element**

It refers to a clickable button on the HTML web page. When the user
clicks the button, the form or inputted data is submitted to the
destination location.

Example for <button> element is:

```
<! DOCTYPE html>

<html>

<head>

<title> Form button element </ title>

<body>

<h4> Form button element </ h4>
```

```
<form action = "/mainpahe.php" method = "POST" >

Type Name Here:

<input name = "username" type = "text" >

<br>

Type Password Here:

<input name = "password" type = "text" >

<br>

<button type = "button" onclick = "submit" >
Submit </ button>

<br>

</ form>

</ body>

</ html>
```

Output:

Form Input Element

Type Name Here: [_____]

Type Password here: [_____]

[Submit]

- **Form <datalist> Element**

It is used to provide a pre-defined list of elements, and the user will have to select one of them.

Example for <datalist> element is:

```
<! DOCTYPE html>

<html>

<head>

<title> Form datalist element </ title>

<body>

<h4> Form datalist element </ h4>

<form action = "/mainpage.php" >

<input list = "cars" >

<datalist id = "cars" >

<option value = "BMW" >

<option value = "Ferrari" >

<option value = "Mercedes" >

<option value = "Toyota" >

<option value = "Honda" >

</ datalist>

<input type = "submit" value = "submit" >

 </form>

</ body>

</ html>
```

Output:

Form datalist Element

Select any from the list: [   ]

Submit input

- **Form <option> Element**

It is used to provide the many options to the user to select one of them based on the information.

Example for <option> element is:

```
<! DOCTYPE html>
<html>
<head>
<title> Form option element </ title>
<body>
<h4> Select your favorite fruit from the list. </
h4>
<select>
<option value = "apple" > Apple </ option>
<option value = "mango" > Mango </ option>
<option value = "grape" > Grape </ option>
<option value = "peach" > Peach </ option>
<option value = "banana" > Banana </ option>
<option value = "orange" > Orange </ option>
```

```
<br>

</ select>

</ body>

</ html>
```

Output:

Select your favorite fruit from the list.

Here the Drop-down list will appear.

- **Form <optgroup> Element**

It is used to group the related options of the same categories.

Example for <optgroup> element is:

```
<! DOCTYPE html>

<html>

<head>

<title> Form optgroup element </ title>

<body>

<h4> Select your favorite fruit or vegetable from
the list. </ h4>

<select>

<optgroup label = "fruits" >

<option value = "apple" > Apple </ option>

<option value = "mango" > Mango </ option>

<option value = "grape" > Grape </ option>
```

```
<option value = "peach" > Peach </ option>

<option value = "banana" > Banana </ option>

<option value = "orange" > Orange </ option>

</ optgroup>

<br>

<optgroup label = "Vegetables" >

<option value = "potato" > Potato </ option>

<option value = "carrot" > Carrot </ option>

<option value = "piece" > Piece </ option>

<option value = "cucumber" > Cucumber </ option>

<option value = "ladyfinger" > Lady Finger </
option>

<option value = "onion" > Onion </ option>

<br>

</ optgroup>

</ select>

</ body>

</ html>
```

Output:

Select your favorite fruit or vegetable from the list.

Here the Drop-down list will appear.

Form Input Types

HTML forms can be used to get multiple types of information from visitors and users. Different form input types that are available in HTML are:

- **Text input**

It is used to take simple text as an input in a single line. Example of text input is:

```
<! DOCTYPE html>
<html>
<head>
<title> Form text input </ title>
<body>
<h4> Form Text Input </ h4>
<form action = "/mainpahe.php" method = "POST" >
Type First Name Here:
<input name = "username" type = "text" >
<br>
Type Last Name Here:
<input name = "lastname" type = "text" >
<br>
</ form>
</ body>
</ html>
```

157

Output:

Form Text Input

Type First Name here: [_____]

Type Last Name here: [_____]

- **Password input**

It is used to input the password in HTML forms. The data typed in password field will be displayed in encrypted form such as asterisk signs instead of actual data. Example for password text input is:

```
<! DOCTYPE html>

<html>

<head>

<title> Form password input </ title>

<body>

<h4> Form Password Input </ h4>

<form action = "/mainpahe.php" method = "POST" >

Type Name Here:

<input name = "username" type = "text" >

<br>

Type Password Here:

<input name = "password" type = "text" >

<br>

</ form>
```

```
</ body>

</ html>
```

Output:

Form Password Input

Type Name Here: _____

Type Password here: _____

- **Submit input**

It is used to submit the entered data into the form. Example for submit input is:

```
<! DOCTYPE html>

<html>

<head>

<title> Form submit input </ title>

<body>

<h4> Form Submit Input </ h4>

<form action = "/mainpahe.php" method = "POST" >

Type First Name Here:

<input name = "username" type = "text" >

<br>

Type Last Name Here:

<input name = "lastname" type = "text" >

<br>
```

```
<input type = "submit" value = "Enter" >

<br>

</ form>

</ body>

</ html>
```

Output:

Form Submit Input

Type First Name here: ▭▭▭▭▭▭▭▭▭▭

Type Last Name here: ▭▭▭▭▭▭▭▭▭▭

| Enter |

- **Reset input**

It is used to clear or reset all the input values in the HTML form. Example for reset input is:

```
<!DOCTYPE html>

<html>

<body>

<h4> Reset Input </ h4>

<p> When user clicks on the reset button all the
entered data will be erased from the fields: </
p>

<form action = "/mainpahe.php" method = "POST" >

Type First Name Here:
```

160

```
<input name = "username" type = "text" >
<br>
Type Last Name Here:
<input name = "lastname" type = "text" >
<br>
<input type = "submit" value = "Enter" >
<br>
<input type = "reset" value = "Reset" >
<br>
</ form>
</ body>
</ html>
```

Output:

Form Submit Input

Type First Name here: [   ]

Type Last Name here: [   ]

| Enter |

| Reset |

• Radio button input

It is used to allow user to select only one from the limited number of available options. Example for radio button is:

```
<! DOCTYPE html>

<html>

<head>

<title> Radio Button Input </ title>

<body>

<h4> Select your favorite fruit from the list. </
h4>

<form action = "/mainpahe.php" method = "POST" >

<input type = "radio" name = "fruit" value =
"Apple" checked> Apple <br>

<input type = "radio" name = "fruit" value =
"Mango" > Mango <br>

<input type = "radio" name = "fruit" value =
"Banana" > Banana <br>

<input type = "radio" name = "fruit" value =
"Orange" > Orange <br>

<input type = "radio" name = "fruit" value =
"Grape" > Grape <br>

</ form>

</ body>

</ html>
```

Output:

Select your favorite fruit from the list.

- o Apple

- o Mango

- o Banana

- o Orange

- o Grape

- **Checkbox input**

It is used when user have to select none or multiple options from the given list. Example for checkbox input is:

```
<! DOCTYPE html>

<html>

<head>

<title> Radio Button Input </ title>

<body>

<h4> Select your favorite fruit from the list. </ h4>

<form action = "/mainpahe.php" method = "POST" >

<input type = "checkbox" name = "fruit" value = "Apple" > Apple <br>
```

```
<input type = "checkbox" name = "fruit1" value =
"Mango" > Mango <br>

<input type = "checkbox" name = "fruit2" value =
"Banana" > Banana <br>

<input type = "checkbox" name = "fruit3" value =
"Orange" > Orange <br>

<input type = "checkbox" name = "fruit4" value =
"Grape" > Grape <br>

</ form>

</ body>

</ html>
```

Output:

Select your favorite fruit from the list.

☐ Apple

☐ Mango

☐ Banana

☐ Orange

☐ Grape

- **Button type input**

It is used to perform some actions regarding to the HTML forms. A tag named as <button> tag is used to create the button on web pages. We must have to attach the function with the button with the help of JavaScript. When user clicks the button, the function attached with the button is performed. Example for button is:

```
<!DOCTYPE html>

<html>

<body>

<h4> Button Input </ h4>

<p> When user clicks on the button attached function will be performed: </ p>

<form action = "/mainpahe.php" method = "POST" >

Type First Name Here:

<input name = "username" type = "text" >

<br>

Type Last Name Here:

<input name = "lastname" type = "text" >

<br>

<button type = "button" onclick = "alert (Congratulations! You have successfully registered.)" > Submit </ button>

</ form>

</ body>

</ html>
```

Output:

When user clicks on the button attached function will be performed:

Type First Name here: ⬚

Type Last Name here: ⬚

| Submit |

- **Color input**

It is used to take favorite color from the user by attaching color picker to the HTML element or field on the web page. Example for the color input is:

```
<! DOCTYPE html>
<html>
<head>
<title> Form color input </ title>
<body>
<h4> Form color picker </ h4>
<p> Click on the field and enter your favorite color. </ p>
<form action = "/mainpahe.php" method = "POST" >
Select from here:
<input type = "color" name = "favoritecolor" value = "#0000ff>
<br>
```

```
<input type = "submit" >
</ form>
</ body>
</ html>
```

Output:

Form color picker

Select from here:

- **Date input**

It is used to add a birthday input field on the web page. Users can input their birth dates or other important dates required in HTML forms. Example for date input is:

```
<! DOCTYPE html>
<html>
<head>
<title> Form date input </ title>
<body>
<h4> Form Date Input Field </ h4>
<form action = "/mainpahe.php" method = "POST" >
Enter your Birth date here:
<input type = "date" name = "bdate" >
<input type = "submit" >
</ form>
```

```
</ body>
</ html>
```

Output:

Form Date Input Field

Enter your Birth date here:

```
mm / day / year
```

```
submit
```

- **Datetime-local input**

It is used to get input by using a date picker on the screen. User can type the date and ty manually or can select it from the date picker wo no time zone it works as local input in HTML. Example for the datetime-local input is:

```
<! DOCTYPE html>
<html>
<head>
<title> Form Datetime-local </ title>
<body>
<h4> Form Datetimo-local Input </ h4>
<form action = "/mainpahe.php" method = "POST" >
Enter your Birth date here:
<input type = "datetime-local" name = "bdatetime"
>
```

```
<input type = "submit" value = "submit" >
</ form>
</ body>
</ html>
```

Output:

Form Datetime-local Input

Enter your Birth date & time here:

mm / day / year

submit

- **Email input**

It is used to get email address in the input field by users or visitors in HTML web pages. When user enters the email some browser automatically validates is it an email address or not by checking the ".com" in the given input. Example for email input is:

```
<! DOCTYPE html>
<html>
<head>
<title> Form Email Input </ title>
<body>
<h4> Form Email Input Field </ h4>
<form action = "/mainpahe.php" method = "POST" >
```

169

```
Enter your E-mail here:

<input type = "email" name = "useremail" >

<input type = "submit" value = "submit" >

</ form>

</ body>

</ html>
```

Output:

Form Datetime-local Input

Enter your E-mail here:

submit

- **Month input**

It is used to get input the month and year from the users. Users can select the month and year from the field according to the requirements of the HTML form. Example for month & year input is:

```
<! DOCTYPE html>

<html>

<head>

<title> Form Month & Year Input </ title>

<body>
```

```
<h4> Form Month Input Field </ h4>
<form action = "/mainpahe.php" method = "POST" >
Enter your Joining Month & Year here:
<input type = "month" name = "userbmonth" >
<input type = "submit" value = "submit" >
</ form>
</ body>
</ html>
```

Output:

Form Month & Year Input Field

Enter your Joining Month & Year here:

mm / year

submit

- **File Input**

It is used to get a file attachment from the visitors. User can browse and upload a file from its computer or mobile storage. Example for file input is:

```
<! DOCTYPE html>
<html>
<head>
<title> Form File Input </ title>
```

```
<body>

<h4> Form File Input Field </ h4>

<form action = "/mainpahe.php" method = "POST" >

Click here to select a file:

<input type = "file" name = "userfile" >

<input type = "submit" value = "submit" >

</ form>

</ body>

</ html>
```

Output:

Form File Input Field

Click here to select a file:

| Browse |

| submit |

- **Number input**

It is used to get a numeric type of input from the users or visitors in HTML forms. We can also restrict the user to enter a number between a specific range. Example for numeric input is:

```
<! DOCTYPE html>

<html>

<head>
```

```
<title> Form Numeric Input </ title>

<body>

<h4> Form Numeric Type Input Field </ h4>

<form action = "/mainpahe.php" method = "POST" >

Enter the number here: (Between 0 - 100)

<input type = "number" name = "usernumber" min =
"0" max = "100" >

<input type = "submit" value = "submit" >

</ form>

</ body>

</ html>
```

Output:

Form Numeric Type Input Field

Enter the number here: (Between 0 – 100)

submit

- **Search input**

It is used to add a search field in HTML forms. It does looks like a simple text fields but acts like a web browser or search engine. Anything user enters will appears in the result of google search. Example for search input is:

```
<! DOCTYPE html>
```

173

```
<html>
<head>
<title> Form Search Input </ title>
<body>
<h4> Form Search Input Field </ h4>
<form action = "/mainpahe.php" method = "POST" >
Google Search:
<input type = "search" name = "gsearch" >
<input type = "submit" value = "submit" >
</ form>
</ body>
</ html>
```

Output:

Form Search Input Field

Google Search:

```
┌─────────────────────────┐
│                         │
└─────────────────────────┘
```

```
┌──────────────┐
│   submit     │
└──────────────┘
```

- **URL input**

It is used to add a URL field in HTML forms. It does looks like a simple text fields but acts like a URL field, some browsers also validate the input whether it is an URL or not by checking the ".com" (domain name) and "https:/" (hypertext transfer protocol) in the given input. Anything user enters will appears in the result of google search. Example for URL input is:

```
<! DOCTYPE html>

<html>

<head>

<title> Form URL Input </ title>

<body>

<h4> Form URL Input Field </ h4>

<form action = "/mainpahe.php" method = "POST" >

Enter your home page address:

<input type = "url" name = "userurl" >

<input type = "submit" value = "submit" >

</ form>

</ body>

</ html>
```

Output:

Form URL Input Field

Enter your home page address:

submit

- **Time input**

It is used to add a time field in our web page. It allows users to add the time in according to the given pattern. Some internet browsers use a time picker to take input from the users with no time zone. Example for time input is:

```
<! DOCTYPE html>
<html>
<head>
<title> Form Time Input </ title>
<body>
<h4> Form Time Input Field </ h4>
<form action = "/mainpahe.php" method = "POST" >
Enter the time here:
<input type = "time" name = "usertime" >
<input type = "submit" value = "submit" >
</ form>
</ body>
</ html>
```

Output:

Form Time Input Field

Enter the time here:

```
-- : -- : --
```

submit

- **Week input**

It is used to add an input field in our web page that will enter the week and year from the visitors. Example for week input is:

```
<! DOCTYPE html>
<html>
<head>
<title> Form Week Input </ title>
<body>
<h4> Form Week & Year Input Field </ h4>
<form action = "/mainpahe.php" method = "POST" >
Enter the Week & Year here:
<input type = "week" name = "userweek" >
<input type = "submit" value = "submit" >
</ form>
</ body>
</ html>
```

Output:

Form Week & Year Input Field

Enter the Week & Year here:

[   ]

[submit]

177

Chapter 13

HTML Class & ID

HTML Class

The word class refers to the template that has some specific information about any object or element. In HTML, classes are the attributes that determine one or more template names for different HTML elements. Classes can be used with any of the HTML elements to describe the same styles and attribute to all of the elements with the same name. Classes are defined in the opening and closing <style> tag. Moreover, we can also use classes with CSS (Cascade Style Sheet) and JavaScript to perform specific operations. Examples of the class are:

- **Class in HTML**

Example of using class attribute for multiple elements by using same class name.

```
<! DOCTYPE html>
<html>
<head>
<title> Class in multiple elements </ title>
<style>
.skill {
Background - color: grey;
```

```
Color: blue;

Font: Comic sans MC;

}

</ style>

</ head>

<body>

<div class = "skill" >

<h3> John </ h3>

<p> John is a Software Engineer and he has
expertise in Web Development. </ p>

</ div>

<div class = "skill" >

<h3> Michael </ h3>

<p> Michael is a Software Engineer and he has
expertise in Desktop Development. </ p>

</ div>

<div class = "skill" >

<h3> Harry </ h3>

<p> Harry is a Software Engineer and he has
expertise in Graphic Design & Game Development.
</ p>

</ div>

<div class = "skill" >

<h3> Smith </ h3>
```

```
<p> Smith is a Software Engineer and he has
expertise in Data Analysis & Network Security. </
p>
</ div>
</ body>
</ html>
```

Output:

John

John is a Software Engineer, and he has expertise in Web Development.

Michael

Michael is a Software Engineer, and he has expertise in Desktop Development.

Harry

Harry is a Software Engineer, and he has expertise in Graphic Design & Game Development.

Smith

Smith is a Software Engineer, and he has expertise in Data Analysis & Network Security.

Example of using classes in inline HTML is:

```
<! DOCTYPE html>

<html>

<head>

<title> Class in multiple elements </ title>

<style>

.skill {

Background - color: grey;

Color: blue;

Font: Comic sans MC;

}

</ style>

</ head>

<body>

<h3 class = "skill" > John </ h3>

<p class = "skill" > John is a Software Engineer
and he has expertise in Web Development. </ p>

<h3 class = "skill" > Michael </ h3>

<p class = "skill" > Michael is a Software
Engineer and he has expertise in Desktop
Development. </ p>

<h3 class = "skill" > Harry </ h3>

<p class = "skill" > Harry is a Software Engineer
and he has expertise in Graphic Design & Game
Development. </ p>
```

```
<h3 class = "skill" > Smith </ h3>

<p class = "skill" > Smith is a Software Engineer
and he has expertise in Data Analysis & Network
Security. </ p>

</ body>

</ html>
```

Output:

John

John is a Software Engineer, and he has expertise in Web Development.

Michael

Michael is a Software Engineer, and he has expertise in Desktop Development.

Harry

Harry is a Software Engineer, and he has expertise in Graphic Design & Game Development.

Smith

Smith is a Software Engineer, and he has expertise in Data Analysis & Network Security.

Example of using multiple classes in inline HTML is:

```
<! DOCTYPE html>

<html>

<head>

<title> Class in multiple elements </ title>

<style>

.skill {

Background - color: grey;

Color: blue;

Font: Comic sans MC;

}

.center {

Text - align: center;

}

</ style>

</ head>

<body>

<h3 class = "skill center" > John </ h3>

<p class = "skill" > John is a Software Engineer
and he has expertise in Web Development. </ p>

<h3 class = "skill center" > Michael </ h3>

<p class = "skill" > Michael is a Software
Engineer and he has expertise in Desktop
Development. </ p>

<h3 class = "skill center" > Harry </ h3>
```

```
<p class = "skill" > Harry is a Software Engineer
and he has expertise in Graphic Design & Game
Development. </ p>

<h3 class = "skill center" > Smith </ h3>

<p class = "skill" > Smith is a Software Engineer
and he has expertise in Data Analysis & Network
Security. </ p>

</ body>

</ html>
```

Output:

John

John is a Software Engineer, and he has expertise in Web Development.

Michael

Michael is a Software Engineer, and he has expertise in Desktop Development.

Harry

Harry is a Software Engineer, and he has expertise in Graphic Design & Game Development.

Smith

Smith is a Software Engineer, and he has expertise in Data Analysis & Network Security.

HTML Id

HTML id is the attribute that is used with elements in with CSS and Java Script to perform specific operations. The main difference between class and id is that class can be used for multiple elements in HTML documents while id is only for a single element. Every element has its unique id and it is written after a # symbol. Example of html id is:

Example of using classes in inline HTML is:

```
<! DOCTYPE html>
<html>
<head>
<title> Class in multiple elements </ title>
<style>
#center {
Text - align: center;
}
.skill {
Background - color: grey;
Color: blue;
Font: Comic sans MC;
}
</ style>
</ head>
<body>
<h3 class = "skill center" > John </ h3>
```

```
<p class = "skill" > John is a Software Engineer
and he has expertise in Web Development. </ p>

<h3 class = "skill" > Michael </ h3>

<p class = "skill" > Michael is a Software
Engineer and he has expertise in Desktop
Development. </ p>

<h3 class = "skill" > Harry </ h3>

<p class = "skill" > Harry is a Software Engineer
and he has expertise in Graphic Design & Game
Development. </ p>

<h3 class = "skill center" > Smith </ h3>

<p class = "skill" > Smith is a Software Engineer
and he has expertise in Data Analysis & Network
Security. </ p>

</ body>

</ html>
```

Output:

John

John is a Software Engineer, and he has expertise in Web Development.

Michael

Michael is a Software Engineer, and he has expertise in Desktop Development.

Harry

Harry is a Software Engineer, and he has expertise in Graphic Design & Game Development.

Smith

Smith is a Software Engineer, and he has expertise in Data Analysis & Network Security.

Example of html id using inline CSS is:

```
<! DOCTYPE html>

<html>

<head>

<title> Class in multiple elements </ title>

</ head>

<body>

<h3 style = "color: red align-text: center" >
John </ h3>

<p style = "color: blue" > John is a Software
Engineer and he has expertise in Web Development.
</ p>

<h3 style = "color: red align-text: center" >
Michael </ h3>

<p style = "color: blue" > Michael is a Software
Engineer and he has expertise in Desktop
Development. </ p>

<h3 style = "color: red align-text: center" >
Harry </ h3>
```

```
<p style = "color: blue" > Harry is a Software
Engineer and he has expertise in Graphic Design &
Game Development. </ p>

<h3 style = "color: red align-text: center" >
Smith </ h3>

<p style = "color: blue" > Smith is a Software
Engineer and he has expertise in Data Analysis &
Network Security. </ p>

</ body>

</ html>
```

Output:

John

John is a Software Engineer, and he has expertise in Web
Development.

Michael

Michael is a Software Engineer, and he has expertise in Desktop
Development.

Harry

Harry is a Software Engineer, and he has expertise in Graphic
Design & Game Development.

Smith

Smith is a Software Engineer, and he has expertise in Data Analysis
& Network Security.

Chapter 14

HTML Multimedia

There are different formats of multimedia that can be used in HTML web pages in different forms. All multimedia files are used to make the web page more user-friendly and help the visitors to understand the content and concepts of the web pages easily. Multimedia used in web pages is music, images, sounds, recordings, videos, animations, etc. Different multimedia formats have different extensions. Some of the common multimedia extensions used in HTML are: .jpg, .jpeg, .mp3, .mp4, WMV, .avi, .mpg, .ogg etc.

HTML Videos

HTML also allows us to add videos on our web pages. Videos are added int our web pages by using an embedded tag named <video>. Video tag has many attributes that have specific tasks. Some of the important video tag attributes are:

- **Controls**

It describes that the browser will allow visitors to use the video controls like play/pause, playback, resume, volume control, etc.

- **Autoplay**

It describes that the video will automatically be played as soon as the browser complete loading data, and the web page is successfully loaded.

- **Height**

This attribute describes what is the height of the video window on the screen using CSS.

- **Loop**

It is a Boolean attribute that describes what the video will automatically seek back to restart when it completes playback.

- **Muted**

It describes that by default, the sound of the video will be silenced until the video is played.

- **Poster**

It is used to display an image or thumbnail while the video is being loaded.

- **Src**

This attribute holds the URL of the video that has to be embedded in the HTML web page. The other option to embed the video is <source> tag; it is used when we used the video that is saved in our server and holds the actual memory address of the video.

- **Preload**

This attribute describes whether the video will be preloaded or not when the web page loaded for the first time. It tells the internet browser about the author's thinking about how the video content will be loaded to get the best user experience.

- **Width**

It is used to describe the width of the video window in pixels on the screen and determined in CSS.

Example of embedding video <source> tag is:

```
<! DOCTYPE html>

<head>

<title> Adding Video in HTML </ title>

</ head>

<body>

<video height = "300" width = "350" controls >

<source src = "myvideo.ogg" type = "video / ogg"
>

<source src = "myvideo.mp4" type = "video / mp4"
>

</ video>

</ body>

</html>
```

Output:

191

Example of embedding video by URL is:

```
<! DOCTYPE html>

<head>

<title> Adding Video in HTML </ title>

</ head>

<body>

<video height = "300" width = "350" controls >

<source src = "myvideo.mp4" type = "video / mp4"
>

<p> If your browser doesn't support the video
here is the link to the video. Click here to
watch the video. </ p>

<a href = http://www.myweb.com/myvideo.mp4 type =
"video / mp4" >

</ video>

</ body>

</html>
```

Output:

If your browser doesn't support the video, here is the link to the video. Click here to watch the video.

http://www.myweb.com/myvideo.mp4

- **<track> tag**

It is used to add the text files or tracks such as subtitles, descriptions, captions, metadata and chapters about the audio and video media. Syntax for <track> tag is: <track src = "address / source of the track file" kind = "type of track file" srclang = "language of the track file" label = " indicates the type of text" >

Example for the <track> tag is:

```
<! DOCTYPE html>

<head>

<title> Adding Video in HTML </ title>

</ head>

<body>

<video height = "300" width = "350" controls >

<source src = "myvideo.mp4" type = "video / mp4"
>

<p> If your browser doesn't support the video
here is the link to the video. Click here to
watch the video. </ p>

<a href = http://www.myweb.com/myvideo.mp4 type =
"video / mp4" >
```

```
<track   src   =   "subtitles_myvideo.vtt"   kind   =
"subtitles" srclang = "en" label = "English" >

<track   src   =   "description_myvideo.vtt"   kind   =
"description" srclang = "en" label = "English" >

<track   src   =   "subtitles_myvideo1.vtt"   kind   =
"subtitles" srclang = "da" label = "Dutch" >

<track   src   =   "chapters_myvideo.vtt"   kind   =
"chapters" srclang = "en" label = "English" >

</ video>

</ body>

</html>
```

Output:

If your browser doesn't support the video, here is the link to the video. Click here to watch the video.

http://www.myweb.com/myvideo.mp4

HTML Audios

HTML allows us to add audio files in our web pages. Audios are added into our web pages by using an embedded tag named <audio>. Everything is written in the opening and closing <audio> tags. The audio tag has many attributes that have specific tasks. Some of the important audio tag attributes are:

- **Controls**

It describes that the browser will allow visitors to use the audio controls like play/pause, playback, resume, volume control, etc.

- **Autoplay**

It describes that the audio will automatically be played as soon as the browser complete loading data, and the web page is successfully loaded.

- **Loop**

It is a Boolean attribute that describes that the audio will automatically seek back to restart when it completes playback.

- **Muted**

It describes that by default, the sound of the audio will be silenced until the audio is played.

- **Src**

This attribute holds the URL of the audio that has to be embedded in the HTML web page. The other option to embed the audio is <source> tag; it is used when we used the audio that is saved in our server and holds the actual memory address of the audio.

- **Preload**

This attribute describes whether the audio will be preloaded or not when the web page loaded for the first time. It tells the internet browser about the author's thinking about how the audio content will be loaded to get the best user experience.

Example of embedding audio by path address:

```
<! DOCTYPE html>
<head>
<title> Adding Audio in HTML </ title>
</ head>
<body>
<audio>
<source src = "myaudio.ogg" type = "audio / ogg"
>
<source src = "myaudio.mp3" type = "audio / mp3"
>
</ audio>
</ body>
</html>
```

Output:

Example of embedding audio by URL is:

```
<! DOCTYPE html>

<head>

<title> Adding Audio in HTML </ title>

</ head>

<body>

<audio>

<source src = "myaudio.mp3" type = "audio / mp3"
>

<p> If your browser doesn't support the audio
here is the link to the audio. Click here to hear
the audio. </ p>

<a href = http://www.myweb.com/myaudio.mp3   type
= "audio / mp3" >

</ audio>

</ body>

</html>
```

Output:

If your browser doesn't support the audio, here is the link to the audio. Click here to hear the audio.

http://www.myweb.com/myaudio.mp3

HTML Plug-ins

Plug-ins are the standard mini-applications that are used to increase the functionality of the internet browser. Plug-ins can be used for multiple purposes, such as displaying maps, verifying bank details, and scanning viruses, etc. Plug-ins can be added by using two tags that are <object> and <embed> tag. Examples of reputed plug-ins are Adobe Flash Player, Java Applet, QuickTime, etc.

- **Adding Plug-in by using <object> tag**

Plug-ins can be added by using <object> tag, it is supported by almost all of the existing internet browsers. Here is the example of adding plug-in by using <object> tag.

```
<! DOCTYPE>
<html>
<head>
<title> Adding Plug-ins </ title>
</ head>
<body>
<object  height  =  "40"  width  =  "200"  data  =
"myplugin.swf" >
</ object>
</ body>
</ html>
```

Output:

198

Here is the example of adding HTML plug-in by using <object> tag.

```
<! DOCTYPE>

<html>

<head>

<title> Adding Plug-ins </ title>

</ head>

<body>

<object height = "40" width = "200" data = "myplugin.html" >

</ object>

</ body>

</ html>
```

Output:

Here the HTML page will shows on the output screen.

- **Adding Plug-in by using <embed> tag**

Second way to add the plug-ins in HTML is by using <embed> tag, it is not supported by all internet browsers. Here is the example of adding plug-in by using <embed> tag.

```
<! DOCTYPE>

<html>

<head>

<title> Adding Plug-ins </ title>

</ head>
```

```
<body>

<embed  height  =  "40"  width  =  "200"  data  =
"myplugin.swf" >

</ body>

</ html>
```

Output:

Adding YouTube Videos

Different browsers use a different type of extensions to play videos. It is complicated and time-consuming to provide all types of extensions of videos to make them play on all the browsers. HTML has an alternative to save your time and efforts in the form of YouTube videos. We can add the YouTube videos by using their id into the HTML web pages. <iframe>, <object>, <embed> tags are used to add the YouTube videos in HTML documents.

- **Adding YouTube by using <iframe>**

```
<! DOCTYPE>

<html>

<head>

<title> Adding YouTube </ title>

</ head>

<body>
```

200

```
<iframe  height  =  "180"  width  =  "200"  src  =
"https:// www. youtube.com /videoid? Autoplay =
1" >

</ body>

</ html>
```

Output:

- **Adding YouTube by using <object>**

```
<! DOCTYPE>

<html>

<head>

<title> Adding YouTube </ title>

</ head>

<body>

<object  height  =  "180"  width  =  "200"  data  =
"https://www.youtube.com/videoid? Autoplay = 1" >

</ object>
```

```
</ body>
</ html>
```

Output:

- **Adding YouTube by using <embed>**

```
<! DOCTYPE>
<html>
<head>
<title> Adding YouTube </ title>
</ head>
<body>
<embed  height  =  "180"  width  =  "200"  src  =
"https://www.youtube.com/videoid? Autoplay = 1" >
</ body>
</ html>
```

Output:

Chapter 15

HTML Graphics

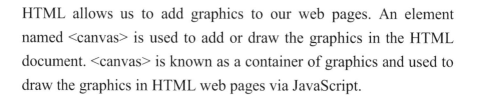

HTML allows us to add graphics to our web pages. An element named <canvas> is used to add or draw the graphics in the HTML document. <canvas> is known as a container of graphics and used to draw the graphics in HTML web pages via JavaScript.

<canvas> is supported by "Google Chrome 4.0", "Microsoft Edge 9.0", "Mozilla Firefox 2.0", "Safari 3.1", and "Opera 9.0". Canvas refers to a rectangular block that has no border or content by default. It has an id that refers to a unique name set by the user and attributes such as style, width, and height.

Examples of drawing graphics from canvas are:

- **Drawing a Rectangle**

```
<! DOCTYPE>

<html>

<head>

<title> Drawing a rectangle </ title>

</ head>

<body>

<canvas id = "myrectangle" height = "180" width =
"200" style = "border : 2px solid #ff0000;" >
```

```
</ canvas>

</ body>

</ html>
```

Output:

- **Drawing a Line**

```
<! DOCTYPE>

<html>

<head>

<title> Drawing a Line </ title>

</ head>

<body>

<canvas id = "myline" height = "180" width =
"200" style = "border : 2px solid #ff0000;" >

</ canvas>

<script>

Variable a = document.getElementById ("myline");

Variable b = a.getContext ("2d");

b.moveTo (0, 0);
```

```
b.lineTo (250, 150);

b.stroke ();

</ script>

</ body>

</ html>
```

Output:

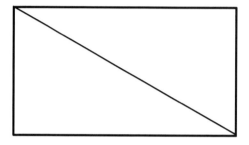

- **Drawing a Circle**

```
<! DOCTYPE>

<html>

<head>

<title> Drawing a Circle </ title>

</ head>

<body>

<canvas id = "mycircle" height - "180" width - "200" style = "border : 2px solid #ff0000;" >

</ canvas>

<script>
```

```
Variable     a     =     document.getElementById
("mycircle");

Variable b = a.getContext ("2d");

b.beginPath ();

b.arc (100, 55, 40, 10, 4*Math.PI);

b.stroke ();

</ script>

</ body>

</ html>
```

Output:

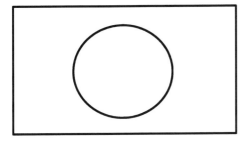

- **Drawing Simple Text**

```
<! DOCTYPE>

<html>

<head>

<title> Drawing the Text </ title>

</ head>

<body>

<canvas id = "mytext" height = "180" width =
"200" style = "border : 2px solid #ff0000;" >

</ canvas>

<script>

Variable a = document.getElementById ("mytext");

Variable b = a.getContext ("2d");

b.font = "40px Times New Roman";

b.fillText ("Welcome", 5, 25);

</ script>

</ body>

</ html>
```

Output:

Welcome

- **Drawing Stroke Text**

```
<! DOCTYPE>

<html>

<head>

<title> Drawing Stroke Text </ title>

</ head>

<body>

<canvas id = "mytext1" height = "180" width =
"200" style = "border : 2px solid #ff0000;" >

</ canvas>

<script>

Variable a = document.getElementById ("mytext1");

Variable b = a.getContext ("2d");

b.font = "40px Times New Roman";

b.strokeText ("Welcome", 5, 25);

</ script>

</ body>

</ html>
```

Output:

209

- **Drawing Linear Gradient**

```
<! DOCTYPE>

<html>

<head>

<title> Drawing Linear Gradient </ title>

</ head>

<body>

<canvas id = "mygradient" height = "180" width =
"200" style = "border : 2px solid #ff0000;" >

</ canvas>

<script>

Variable     a     =     document.getElementById
("mygradient");

Variable b = a.getContext ("2d");

// here we create the gradient

Variable g = b.createLinearGradient (10, 10, 150,
10);

g.addColorStop (10, "red");

g.addColorStop (20, "white");

// here we fill the box with gradient

b.fillStyle = g;

b.fillRect (20, 20, 200, 100);

</ script>

</ body>

</ html>
```

210

Output:

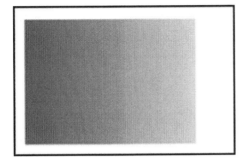

- **Drawing Circular Gradient**

```
<! DOCTYPE>

<html>

<head>

<title> Drawing Linear Gradient </ title>

</ head>

<body>

<canvas id = "mygradient" height = "180" width =
"200" style = "border : 2px solid #ff0000;" >

</ canvas>

<script>

Variable     a     =     document.getElementById
("mygradient");

Variable b = a.getContext ("2d");

// here we create the gradient

Variable g = b.createRadialGradient (90, 60, 5,
100, 90, 60);
```

```
g.addColorStop (10, "red");
g.addColorStop (20, "white");
// here we fill the box with gradient
b.fillStyle = g;
b.fillRect (20, 20, 200, 100);
</ script>
</ body>
</ html>
```

Output:

- **Drawing an Image**

```
<! DOCTYPE>
<html>
<head>
<title> Drawing Linear Gradient </ title>
</ head>
<body>
// here is the image to be filled in the canvas
<p> We have to fill this image in the canvas. </ p>
<img id = "myphoto" src = "/assets /images /myphoto.png" alt = "photo" Height = "250" width = "200" >
<p> Here is the canvas to fill. </ p>
<canvas id = "myphoto" height = "180" width = "200" style = "border : 2px solid #ff0000;" >
</ canvas>
<p> <button> onclick = "myphoto()" > Click here </ button> </ p>
<script>
Function myphoto () {
Variable     a     =     document.getElementById ("myphoto");
Variable b = a.getContext ("2d");
Variable     img     =     document.getElementById ("photo");
b.drawImage (img, 5, 5);
}
```

```
</ script>
</ body>
</ html>
```

Output:

We have to fill this image on the canvas.

Here is the canvas to fill.

After clicking the button, the image will be displayed inside the canvas

Chapter 16

HTML Frames & iFrames

HTML Frames

Frame refers to the individual parts or blocks of the web pages and used to split the browser window into sections. Frames divide the browser window in the form of rows and columns. Multiple frames are combined to create a frameset. A tag named <frame> is used to create frames in the HTML document. Different <frame> tags are combined and written in the <frameset> tag. The <frameset> tag is written in opening and closing <body> tag.

Attributes of the <frame> tag are rows and cols that defines every individual frame in the frameset. There are some disadvantages of frames in HTML that are: Smaller mobiles do not support frames because their small screen is not able to divide all the frames accurately. Web pages that are created by framesets are not correctly displayed on different screens due to the different screen resolutions. Some browsers do not support the frames.

Attributes of the <frameset> tag are:

- **rows**

It is used to describe the rows of frames in the frameset. If we want to create five frames in the frameset, then we can define the height of each row in the frameset.

- **cols**

It is used to describe how many columns will be in the frameset, and it also defines the width of each column.

- **border**

It is used to define the width of each border in terms of pixels for all frames in the frameset.

- **framespacing**

It is used to define the space between each frame in the frameset in terms of pixels.

- **frameborder**

It is a Boolean attribute and used to define whether the three-dimensional border in each frame will be displayed or not.

Attributes of the <frame> tag are:

- **name**

It is used to assign a user-defined name to the frame. It is used to link multiple frames with each other and to tell the browser which document should be opened in the described frame.

- **src**

It is used to assign the file name in the form of a URL that has to be loaded in the current frame.

- **marginwidth**

It is used to define the space and width between the frame borders and content.

- **frameboeder**

It acts as a Boolean attribute and used to define whether the border of each frame will be displayed or not. It takes only "o" or "1" to define the border around the frames.

- **Marginheight**

It is used to define the space and height between the upper and lower frame borders and content.

- **scrolling**

It is used to set the scroll bar in the frames. It acts as a Boolean attribute and takes only "0" or "1". If the value of the scrolling attribute is "1" than the frame will have the scroll bar.

- **longdesc**

It refers to the long description of the frame content. It is used to add a link to another web page in the frame that holds the detailed description of the existing frame.

- **noresize**

It is used to allow or prevent the visitor from resizing the frames in the browser window. By default, it is set to allow users to resize the frames to view the content in the frames accurately.

Examples of creating frameset and frame in HTML are:

```
<! DOCTYPE html>

<html>

<head>

<title> Creating HTML Frames </ title>

</ head>

<frameset cols = "30, 20, 20, 30" >

<frame name = "first" src = "/html /frames
/first.html" />

<frame name = "second" src = "/html /frames
/second.html" />

<frame name = "third" src = "/html /frames
/third.html" />

<frame name = "forth" src = "/html /frames
/forth.html" />

<! -- if the current browser version does not
support the frames then this message will be
displayed on the screen. -->
```

```
<noframes>

<body> This browser does not support the frames
technology. </ body>

</ noframes>

</ frameset>

</ html>
```

Output:

The above code will create four frames in the browser window and display the linked web pages in the frames. Try this code by creating the web pages first to get the proper understanding of the concept.

Another example of frames using target attribute:

```
// it is the first file which describes the
frameset.

// Name this file as "mainfile.html"

<! DOCTYPE html>

<html>

<head>

<title> Creating HTML Frames </ title>

</ head>

<frameset cols = "30, 70" >

<frame name = "first" src = "/html /frames
/header.html" />

<frame name = "second" src = "/html /frames
/body.html" />
```

```html
<! -- if the current browser version does not
support the frames then this message will be
displayed on the screen. -->

<noframes>

<body> This browser does not support the frames
technology. </ body>

</ noframes>

</ frameset>

</ html>

// Now create another file which links the other
files to the frames.

// name this file as a header file

<! DOCTYPE html>

<html>

<head>

<title> Creating HTML Head File </ title>

</ head>

<body>

<a href = "https://www.facebook.com" target =
"first" > Facebook </ a>

<br />

<br />

<a href = "https://www.youtube.com" target =
"first" > YouTube </ a>

<br />

<br />
```

```
<a href = "https://www.twitter.com" target =
"first" > Twitter </ a>

<br />

</ body>

</ html>

// Create the file for the second frame

// link this file with the second frame in target
attribute

<! DOCTYPE html>

<html>

<head>

<title> Creating HTML Content File </ title>

</ head>

<body>

<p> When you click any link in the first frame
content of the link will be displayed in this
frame. </ p>

</ body>

</ html>
```

Output:

The above code will create two frames in the browser window first
frame will have the links and second frame will display the content
of all the associated links. Try this code by creating the web pages
first to get the proper understanding of the concept.

HTML iframes

<iframe> tag is used to display the browser windows within another window. It is used to create inline <frame> tags in HTML document. It will display a separate browser window within the existing window with complete headers and the body of the web page.

Attributes of the <iframe> tag are:

- **name**

It is used to assign a user-defined name to the frame. It is used to link multiple frames with each other and to tell the browser which document should be opened in the described frame.

- **src**

It is used to assign the file name in the form of a URL that has to be loaded in the current frame.

- **marginwidth**

It is used to define the space and width between the frame borders and content.

- **frameborder**

It acts as a Boolean attribute and used to define whether the border of each frame will be displayed or not. It takes only "o" or "1" to define the border around the frames.

- **margin height**

It is used to define the space and height between the upper and lower frame borders and content.

- **scrolling**

It is used to set the scroll bar in the frames. It acts as a Boolean attribute and takes only "0" or "1". If the value of the scrolling attribute is "1" than the frame will have the scroll bar.

- **longdesc**

It refers to the long description of the frame content. It is used to add a link to another web page in the frame that holds the detailed description of the existing frame.

- **height**

It is used to define the height of the <iframe> tag.

- **width**

It is used to define the width of the <iframe> tag.

Examples of the <iframe> tag are:

```
<! DOCTYPE html>

<html>

<head>

<title> Creating HTML iframes </ title>

</ head>

<body>

<iframe width = "80%" height = "500px" name =
"main file" src = "main.html" >

</ iframe>

<p> <a href = "https://mywebsite.com" target =
"main file" > My Website </ a> </ p>
```

```
<p> When the user clicks on the link the web
pages linked in the iframe will be displayed in
the frame body. </ p>

</ body>

</ html>
```

Output:

The above code will create an iframe in the browser window first
frame when visitor clicks on the link the web page will be displayed
inside the frame body. Try this code by creating the web pages first
to get the proper understanding of the concept.

Chapter 17

Advanced HTML Features

This chapter includes the advanced features and concepts of HTML development. You have learned all the basic tags and concepts of Hypertext Markup Language in the previous chapters. Advanced features of HTML will assist you in making your web pages more creative, good-looking, user-friendly and responsive.

HTML Marquees

Marquees in HTML are used to scroll all types of content on web pages such as text, images, and animations. It is used to move the content from upside-down vertically and from left to right and right to left horizontally. We use the <marquee> tag to scroll the content.

Attributes of <marquee> tag are:

- **height**

It is used to define the height of the marquee. For example, 20 or 30% of the browser window.

- **width**

It is used to define the width of the marquee. For example, 40 or 60% of the browser window.

- **direction**

It is used to define the direction of the content scrolling on the browser screen. For example, from top to bottom, from bottom to top, from left to right, and from right to left.

- **behavior**

It is used to define the scroll type on the browser screen. For example, scrolling, sliding, and alternating of the content.

- **scrolldelay**

It is used to define how long will it wait after each scroll loop.

- **scrollamount**

It is used to define the speed of scrolling of the content on the browser screen.

- **loop**

Loop attribute defines how many times the marquee tag will be executed. The default value of the marquee tag is infinite, but the user can change it.

- **hspace**

hspace attribute is used to define the horizontal space around the content of the marquee tag.

- **vspace**

The vspace attribute is used to define the vertical space around the content of the marquee tag.

- **bgcolor**

It is used to define the background color of the scrolling content.

Examples to understand the working of marquee tag are:

```
// Example of simple <marquee> tag
<!DOCTYPE html>
<html>
<head>
<title> Marquee Tag in HTML </ title>
</ head>
<body>
<marquee> My name is John. </ marquee>
</ body>
</ html>
```

Output:

The text written in the marquee tag will scroll from left to right on the full screen. For better understanding try it by yourself.

```
// Example of <marquee> tag using half screen of
the browser

<!DOCTYPE html>

<html>

<head>

<title> Marquee Tag in HTML </ title>

</ head>

<body>

<marquee  width  =  "50%"  >  My  name  is  John.  </
marquee>

</ body>

</ html>
```

Output:

The text written in the marquee tag will scroll from left to right on the half screen. For better understanding try it by yourself.

```
// Example of <marquee> tag scrolling right to
left

<!DOCTYPE html>

<html>

<head>

<title> Marquee Tag in HTML </ title>

</ head>

<body>

<marquee width = "50%" direction = "right" > My
name is John. </ marquee>

</ body>

</ html>
```

Output:

The text written in the marquee tag will scroll from right to left on the half screen. For better understanding try it by yourself.

HTML Layouts

HTML layouts are used to make the web page more attractive and user-friendly. Layouts in web development is an essential component of designing that is referred to as the arrangement of different elements on the HTML page. A complete web page layout consists of the following parts: Header, Navigation Bar, Index, Content Area, Article, Section and Footer.

Basic Structure of HTML Layout is:

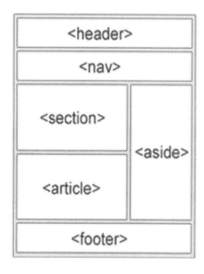

HTML allows us to create attractive layouts by using multiple techniques. That techniques are:

- Layouts by using HTML Tables

- Layouts by using <div> or <span>

- Layouts by using CSS Floats

- Layouts by using CSS Flexbox

Layouts by using HTML Tables

HTML layouts can be created by using table tags. But it is the earliest and backward method of designing layouts in HTML, and it does take a lot of time. We use <table> tag to create rows and columns and use some CSS properties to engage them all to build the complete web page layout.

Example for creating layout by using <table> with single column is:

```
<!DOCTYPE html>

<html>

<head>

<title> Example of creating Layout using Tables
</ title>

</ head>

<body>

<table width = "100%" border = "1px" >

<tr>

<td colspan = "3" bgcolor = "#00FF00" > <center>

<h1> This is the header of the web page </h1> </
center>

</ td>

</ tr>

<tr align = "top" >

<td bgcolor = "#C0C0C0" width = "35" > This is
the Menu bar of the HTML Web page <br /> <br />
```

```html
<a href = "/assets /web_pages /c++.html" > C++ </
a> <br />

<a href = "/assets /web_pages /html_book.html" >
HTML </ a> <br />

<a href = "/assets /web_pages /php_book.html" >
PHP </ a> <br />

<a href = "/assets /web_pages /python_book.html"
> PYTHON </ a> <br />

</ td>

<td bgcolor = "#00FF55" width = "70" height =
"150"> This is the main body or the content area
of the Web page. </ td>

</ tr>

<tr>

<td colspan = "3" bgcolor = "#00FF00"> <center>
This is the footer of the web page </ center> </
td>

</ tr>

</ table>

</ body>

</ html>
```

Output:

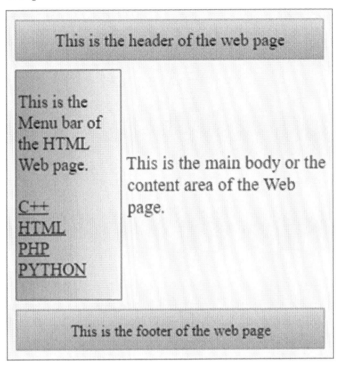

Example of using different columns in web page layout:

```
<!DOCTYPE html>

<html>

<head>

<title> Example of creating Layout using Tables
</ title>

</ head>

<body>

<table width = "100%" border = "1px" >

<tr>

<td colspan = "3" bgcolor = "#00FF00" > <center>
```

```html
<h1> This is the header of the web page </h1> </
center>

</ td>

</ tr>

<tr align = "top" >

<td bgcolor = "#C0C0C0" width = "25" > This is
the Menu bar of the HTML Web page <br /> <br />

<a href = "/assets /web_pages /c++.html" > C++ </
a> <br />

<a href = "/assets /web_pages /html_book.html" >
HTML </ a> <br />

<a href = "/assets /web_pages /php_book.html" >
PHP </ a> <br />

<a href = "/assets /web_pages /python_book.html"
> PYTHON </ a> <br />

</ td>

<td bgcolor = "#00FF55" width = "50" height =
"100"> This is the main body or the content area
of the Web page. </ td>

</ tr>

<tr align = "top" >

<td bgcolor = "#C0C0C0" width = "25" > This is
the Menu bar of the HTML Web page <br /> <br />

<a href = "/assets /web_pages /c++.html" > C++ </
a> <br />

<a href = "/assets /web_pages /html_book.html" >
HTML </ a> <br />
```

```
<a href = "/assets /web_pages /php_book.html" >
PHP </ a> <br />

<a href = "/assets /web_pages /python_book.html"
> PYTHON </ a> <br />

</ td>

<tr>

<td colspan = "3" bgcolor = "#00FF00"> <center>
This is the footer of the web page </ center> </
td>

</ tr>

</ table>

</ body>

</ html>
```

Output:

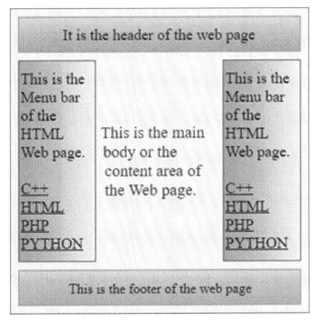

Layouts by using <div> or <span>

We can also create user-friendly and responsive HTML layouts by using <div> or <span> tags. These tags are more efficient way to create web pages layouts than tables. It uses CSS properties to make the web page responsive on all type of browsers.

Example of creating layout by using <div> tag:

```
<! DOTYPE html>

<html>

<head>

<title> Example of creating layouts by using
<div> tag </ title>

</ head>

<body>

<div style = "width: 90%" >

<div style = "width: 85%; background-color:
#00FF00;" > <center>

<h3> This is the header of the web page </ h3> </
center>

</ div>

<div style = "width: 120px; height: 30px;
background-color: #00CC00; float: left;" >

<div> This is the menu bar of the HTML web page.
</ div>

<a href = "/assets /web_pages /c++.html" > C++ </
a> <br />
```

```
<a href = "/assets /web_pages /html_book.html" >
HTML </ a> <br />

<a href = "/assets /web_pages /php_book.html" >
PHP </ a> <br />

<a href = "/assets /web_pages /python_book.html"
> PYTHON </ a> <br />

</ div>

<div style = "width: 120px; height: 30px;
background-color: #00CC00;" >

<center> This is the footer of the web page </
center>

</ div>

</ div>

</ body>

</ html>
```

Output:

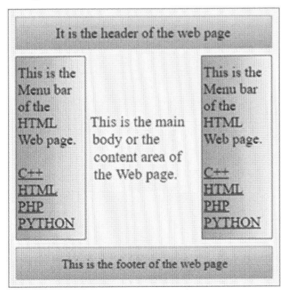

237

Another example of creating layouts by using proper CSS designing:

```
<! DOCTYPE html>

<html>

<head>

<title> Example of creating layout by using <div>
tag and CSS </ title>

<style>

.header {

Background-color: #00FF00;

font-weight: italic;

font-size: 30px;

}

.header1 {

Background-color: #00CC00;

margin-bottom: 10px;

margin-left: 5px;

font-size: 15px;

}

.b {

margin: auto;

background-color: #00CC00;

background-position: center;

}

.menubar {
```

```css
top: 0;

background-color: #00FF00;

padding: 20px 10px 20px 10px;

color: blue;

margin: auto;

}

.menubar1 {

float: right;

color: blue;

margin: auto;

}

.footer {

width: 95%;

bottom: 5px;

background-color: #00FF00;

font-weight: italic;

font-size: 30px;

padding-top: 5px;

padding-bottom: 5px;

text-align: center;

}

</ style>

</ head>

<body>
```

```html
<!-- Header of the Web Page -->

<header>

<div class = "header"> My Website </ div>

<div class = "header1"> A platform to learn all
programming languages. </ div>

</ header>

<!-- Menu Bar of the Web Page -->

<div class = "menubar">

<a href = "#main"> HOME PAGE </ a>

<a href = "#updates"> UPDATES </ a>

<a href = "#announcements"> ANNOUNCEMENTS </ a>

<div class = "menubar1">

<a href = "#signin"> SIGNIN </ a>

</ div>

</ div>

<!-- Body of the layout starts from here -->

<div>

<h3> This is the main body or content area of the
web page. </ h3>

</ div>

<!-- Footer of the layout starts from here -->

<footer> This is the footer of the web page </
footer>

</ body>

</ html>
```

Output:

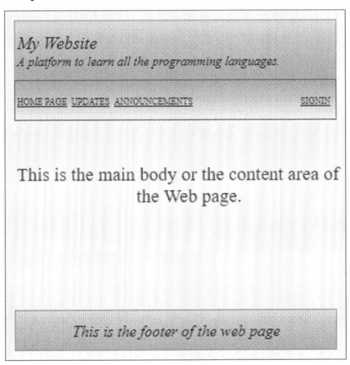

Layouts by using CSS Floats

It is the most common and easiest way of creating HTML layouts. We have to float and clear the CSS properties to create the HTML web layouts. Example for CSS Float Layout is:

```
<! DOCTYPE html>

<html>

<head>

<title> CSS Floats Layout </ title>

<style>
```

```css
* {
box-sizing: border-box;
}
body {
font-family: Times New Romans, Arial, Calibri;
}
header {
background-color: #C0C0C0;
padding: 10px;
text-align: center;
text-weight: italic;
font-size: 20px;
color: blue;
}
nav {
text-align: center;
width: 40%;
height: 250px;
background-color: #00FF00;
padding: 10px;
}
body {
text-align: center;
padding: 10px;
```

```
width: 60%;

background-color: #C0C0C0;

height: 150px;

}

footer {

background-color: #00FF00;

padding: 5px;

text-align: center;

text-weight: italic;

color: blue;

}

</ style>

</ head>

<body>

<header>

 <h3> My Website </ h3>

</ header>

<section>

<nav>

<ul>

<li> <a href = "/web /c++.html"> C++ </ a> </ li>

<li><a href="/web /main.html"> HTML </ a> </ li>

<li><a href="/web /php.html"> PHP </ a> </ li>

</ ul>
```

```
</ nav>

<article>

<h3> CSS Float Layouts</ h3>

<p>Hey! <br /> My name is John. I'm a software
engineer. I have expertise in: <br /> C++ <br />
Web Development <br /> Network Security <br />
Game Development <br /> Graphic Design </ p>

   </ article>

</ section>

<footer>

<p> This is the footer of the web page </ p>

</ footer>

</ body>

</ html>
```

Output:

Layouts by using CSS Flexbox

Second way of designing the responsive and user-friendly HTML layouts id by using CSS Flexbox properties. Example of CSS Flexbox is:

It is the most common and easiest way of creating HTML layouts. We have to float and clear the CSS properties to create the HTML web layouts. Example for CSS Float Layout is:

```
<! DOCTYPE html>

<html>

<head>

<title> CSS Floats Layout </ title>

<style>

* {

box-sizing: border-box;

}

body {

font-family: Times New Romans, Arial, Calibri;

}

header {

background-color: #C0C0C0;

padding: 10px;

text-align: center;

text-weight: italic;

font-size: 20px;
```

245

```css
color: blue;
}
section {
display: -webkit-flex;
display: flex;
}
nav {
-webkit-flex: 1;
-ms-flex: 1;
flex: 1;
background: #C0C0C0;
padding: 10px;
}
body {
text-align: center;
padding: 10px;
width: 60%;
background-color: #C0C0C0;
height: 150px;
}
footer {
background-color: #00FF00;
padding: 5px;
text-align: center;
```

```
text-weight: italic;

color: blue;

}

</ style>

</ head>

<body>


<header>
 <h3> My Website </ h3>
</ header>

<section>

<nav>

<ul>

<li> <a href = "/web /c++.html"> C++ </ a> </ li>

<li><a href="/web /main.html"> HTML </ a> </ li>

<li><a href="/web /php.html"> PHP </ a> </ li>

</ ul>

</ nav>

<article>

<h3> CSS Float Layouts</ h3>

<p>Hey! <br /> My name is John. I'm a software
engineer. I have expertise in: <br /> C++ <br />
Web Development <br /> Network Security <br />
Game Development <br /> Graphic Design </ p>

  </ article>
```

```
</ section>

<footer>

<p> This is the footer of the web page </ p>

</ footer>

</ body>

</ html>
```

Output:

HTML Computer Code

It is known as a phrase tag and used to display the messages related to computer codes in a unique and formatted way on the screen. All the computer code content is written within the opening and closing <code> tag. Example of displaying computer code on the Web page is:

```
<! DOCTYPE html>

<html>

<head>

<title> Example of Computer Code </ title>

</ head>

<body>

<h3> Displaying Computer Code </ h3>

<p> Here is the computer programming code: </ p>

<code>

a = 2; <br />

b = 5; <br />

c = a * b;

</ code>

</ body>

</ html>
```

Output:

Displaying Computer Code

Here is the computer programming code:

a = 2;

b = 5;

c = a * b;

Another example of displaying computer code with attributes on the Web page is:

```
<! DOCTYPE html>
<html>
<head>
<title> Example of Computer Code </ title>
</ head>
<body>
<h3 style = "color: blue" > Displaying Computer
Code </ h3>
<p style = "color: red" > Here is the computer
programming code: </ p>
<code>
variable = 20; <br />
variable1 = 50; <br />
product = variable * variable1;
```

```
</ code>
</ body>
</ html>
```

Output:

Displaying Computer Code

Here is the computer programming code:

variable = 20;

variable1 = 50;

product = variable * variable1;

HTML Charset

It is used to tell the browser the characters type used in the HTML web page. HTML charset is very important to load the HTML page accurately. Charset attribute is defined inside the <meta> tag. Syntax for the Charset attribute is:

<meta charset = "character set name" >

Different types of character sets used in HTML are:

- **The ASCII Charset**

The ASCII values for the control characters are from 0 to 31. 32 to 126 are reserved for the letters, symbols, and digits. The ASCII character set does not use values higher than 127.

251

- **The ANSII Charset**

ANSII character set has the same values from 0 to 126 as the ASCII charset. From 128 to 159 are reserved for the proprietary characters. Values from 160 to 255 are the same as the UTF-8 character set.

- **The ISO-8859-1 Charset**

The ISO-8859-1 values from 0 to 127 are the same as the ASCII character set values. The ISO-8859-1 character set does not use values from 128 to 159. Values from 160 to 255 are the same as UTF-8.

- **The UTF-8 Charset**

The values in UTF-8 from 0 to 127 are the same as the ASCII character set. It does not use values from 128 to 159. From 160 to 255 are the same as both of the ANSII and ISO-8859-1. But it continues from 256 and has more than 10,000 different characters. Here is the detailed list of UTF-8 characters used in HTML.

Mathematical Operators used in HTML

Character	Name	Decimal Value	Hex Value	Entity
∀	All	8704	2200	&forall;
∁	Complement	8705	2201	
∂	Partial Differential	8706	2202	&part;
∃	There Exists	8707	2203	&exist;
∄	There Does Not Exist	8708	2204	

∅	Empty Set	8709	2205	&empty;
Δ	Increment	8710	2206	
∇	Nabla	8711	2207	&nabla;
∈	Element Of Operator	8712	2208	&isin;
∉	Not an Element Of operator	8713	2209	&notin;
∊	Small Element Operator	8714	220A	
∋	Contains as Member	8715	220B	&ni;
∌	Does Not Contains as Member	8716	220C	
∍	Small Contains as Member Operator	8717	220D	
∎	End of Proof Sign	8718	220E	
∏	N-Array Product Sign	8719	220F	&prod;
∐	N-Array Coproduct Sign	8720	2210	
Σ	N-Array Summation Sign	8721	2211	&sum;
−	Minus Sign	8722	2212	&minus;
∓	Minus-or-Plus Sign	8723	2213	
∔	Dot-Plus Sign	8724	2214	
∕	Division or Slash Sign	8725	2215	
∖	Set Minus Sign	8726	2216	
∗	Asterisk Sign	8727	2217	&lowast;
∘	Ring Operator Sign	8728	2218	

·	Bullet Operator Sign	8729	2219	
√	Square Root Operator	8730	221A	&radic;
∛	Cube Root Operator	8731	221B	
∜	Fourth Root Operator	8732	221C	
∝	Proportional to Operator	8733	221D	&prop;
∞	Infinity Sign	8734	221E	&infin;
∟	Right Angle Operator	8735	221F	
∠	Angle Operator	8736	2220	&ang;
∡	Measured Angle Operator	8737	2221	
∢	Spherical Angle Operator	8738	2222	
∣	Divides Operator	8739	2223	
∤	Does not Divides Operator	8740	2224	
∥	Parallel to Operator	8741	2225	
∦	Not Parallel to Operator	8742	2226	
∧	Logical And Operator	8743	2227	&and;
∨	Logical Or Operator	8744	2228	&or;
∩	Intersection Operator	8745	2229	&cap;
∪	Union Operator	8746	222A	&cup;
∫	Integral Operator	8747	222B	&int;
∬	Double integral Operator	8748	222C	

∭	Triple Integral Operator	8749	222D	
∮	Contour Integral Operator	8750	222E	
∯	Surface Integral Operator	8751	222F	
∰	Volume Integral Operator	8752	2230	
∱	Clock-wise Integral operator	8753	2231	
∲	Clock-wise Contour Integral Opt	8754	2232	
∳	Anti-clockwise Contour Integral Opt	8755	2233	
∴	Therefore Operator	8756	2234	&there4;
∵	Because of Operator	8757	2235	
∶	Ratio Operator	8758	2236	
∷	Proportion Operator	8759	2237	
∸	Dot-minus Operator	8760	2238	
∹	Excess Operator	8761	2239	
∺	Geometric Proportion Operator	8762	223A	
∻	Homothetic Operator	8763	223B	
∼	Tilde Sign	8764	223C	&sim;
∽	Reversed Tilde Sign	8765	223D	
∾	Inverted Lazy S Operator	8766	223E	
∿	Sine Wave Operator	8767	223F	

≀	Wreath Product Operator	8768	2240	
≁	Not Tilde Sign	8769	2241	
≂	Minus Tilde Operator	8770	2242	
≃	Asymptotically Equal to Operator	8771	2243	
≄	Not Asymptotically Equal to Opt	8772	2244	
≅	Approximately Equal to Operator	8773	2245	&cong;
≆	Approximately but not Equal to Opt	8774	2246	
≇	Neither Approximately nor Equal to	8775	2247	
≈	Almost Equal to Operator	8776	2248	&asymp;
≉	Not Almost Equal to Operator	8777	2249	
≊	Almost Equal to Operator	8778	224A	
≋	Triple Tilde Sign	8779	224B	
≌	All Equal to Operator	8780	224C	
≍	Equivalent Operator	8781	224D	
≎	Geometrically Equivalent to Opt	8782	224E	
≏	Difference Operator	8783	224F	
≐	Approaches the Limit operator	8784	2250	
≑	Geometrically Equal	8785	2251	

	Operator			
≒	Image of Operator	8786	2252	
≓	Approximately Equal to operator	8787	2253	
:=	Colon Equals Operator	8788	2254	
=:	Equals Colon Operator	8789	2255	
≖	Ring in Equal to Operator	8790	2256	
≗	Ring Equal to Operator	8791	2257	
≘	Corresponds to Operator	8792	2258	
≙	Estimate Operator	8793	2259	
≚	Equiangular Operator	8794	225A	
≛	Stars Equal Operator	8795	225B	
≜	Delta Equals to Operator	8796	225C	
≝	Equal by Definition Operator	8797	225D	
≞	Measured by Operator	8798	225E	
≟	Questioned Equal to Operator	8899	225F	
≠	Not Equal to Operator	8800	2260	&ne;
≡	Identical to Operator	8801	2261	&equiv;
≢	Not Identical to Operator	8802	2262	

XHTML

XHTML stands for "Extensive Hypertext Markup Language" belongs to the family of XML languages. XHTML is almost a replica of HTML and has more validations than HTML. In the present era, we can find a lot of Internet Browsers on the web.

Some browsers support only system computers; some support mobile and other devices. Because mobile phones and other smaller devices are unable to load all resources and data present on the web page. So, XHTML is used for the markup of all types of web pages correctly to run on all types of devices. It is supported by all good internet browsers in the world.

Differences in XHTML form XHTML

The major differences between HTML and XHTML are as follows:

- <! DOCTYPE> tag is compulsory to include in XHTML.

Example of describing the <! DOCTYPE> tag in XHTML is:

```
<! DOCTYPE html Public "-//MWEB//ABC XHTML 1.0
Transitional // EN" "https:// www. Myweb.com /TR
/XHTML /ABC /XHTML1tTransitional.aBC" >

<html>

<head>

<title> XHTML Example </ title>

</ head>

<body>

<p> My name is John and I'm a software engineer.
I have expertise in Web Development, C++
```

```
Development, Game Development, Graphic Designing,
and Game Development. </ p>

</ body>

</ html>
```

Output:

My name is John and I'm a software engineer. I have expertise in Web Development, C++ Development, Game Development, Graphic Designing, and Game Development.

- Other compulsory tags included <html>, <head>, <title>, and <body> tags.

```
Example of describing the <! DOCTYPE> tag in
XHTML is:

<! DOCTYPE html Public "-//MWEB//ABC XHTML 1.0
Transitional // EN" "https:// www. Myweb.com /TR
/XHTML /ABC /XHTML1tTransitional.aBC" >

<html xmlns = "https: // www. Myweb.com //2019
/xhtml" >

<head>

<title> XHTML Example </ title>

</ head>

<body>

<p> My name is John and I'm a software engineer.
I have expertise in Web Development, C++
Development, Game Development, Graphic Designing,
and Game Development. </ p>
```

```
</ body>

</ html>
```

Output:

My name is John, and I'm a software engineer. I have expertise in Web Development, C++ Development, Game Development, Graphic Designing, and Game Development.

- Elements in XHTML must always be nested appropriately.

Example of nesting the elements properly in XHTML is:

```
<! DOCTYPE html Public "-//MWEB//ABC XHTML 1.0
Transitional // EN" "https:// www. Myweb.com /TR
/XHTML /ABC /XHTML1tTransitional.aBC" >

<html xmlns = "https: // www. Myweb.com //2019
/xhtml" >

<head>

<title> XHTML Example </ title>

</ head>

<body>

//Here we have nested all the elements properly
in XHTML Document

<p> My name is John and I'm a software engineer.
I have expertise in <b> Web Development, C++
Development, Game Development, Graphic Designing,
and Game Development. </b> </ p>

</ body>

</ html>
```

260

Output:

My name is John and I'm a software engineer. I have expertise in **Web Development, C++ Development, Game Development, Graphic Designing, and Game Development.**

- All the elements must be in lowercase letters & closed in XHTML.

Example of writing all tags in lowercase and closed properly in XHTML document is:

```
<! DOCTYPE html Public "-//MWEB//ABC XHTML 1.0
Transitional // EN" "https:// www. Myweb.com /TR
/XHTML /ABC /XHTML1tTransitional.aBC" >

<html xmlns = "https: // www. Myweb.com //2019
/xhtml" >

<head>

<title> XHTML Example </ title>

</ head>

<body>

<p> My name is John and I'm a software engineer.
I have expertise in Web Development, C++
Development, Game Development, Graphic Designing,
and Game Development. </ p>

</ body>

</ html>
```

Output:

My name is John and I'm a software engineer. I have expertise in Web Development, C++ Development, Game Development, Graphic Designing, and Game Development.

In the above example, each element has a proper closing tag.

- Every XHTML document must have at least one root element in the web page.

Example of describing the root in XHTML is:

```
<! DOCTYPE html Public "-//MWEB//ABC XHTML 1.0
Transitional // EN" "https:// www. Myweb.com /TR
/XHTML /ABC /XHTML1tTransitional.aBC" >

<html xmlns = "https: // www. Myweb.com //2019
/xhtml" >

<head>

<title> XHTML Example </ title>

</ head>

<body>

<p> My name is John and I'm a software engineer.
I   have   expertise   in   Web   Development,   C++
Development, Game Development, Graphic Designing,
and Game Development. </ p>

</ body>

</ html>
```

Output:

My name is John and I'm a software engineer. I have expertise in Web Development, C++ Development, Game Development, Graphic Designing, and Game Development.

Above example have more than one root element. Root elements are <html>, <head>, <body>, etc.

- All attributes in XHTML must be in lowercase letters, adequately quoted, and minimized.

Example of describing the attributes in XHTML is:

```
<! DOCTYPE html Public "-//MWEB//ABC XHTML 1.0
Transitional // EN" "https:// www. Myweb.com /TR
/XHTML /ABC /XHTML1tTransitional.aBC" >

<html xmlns = "https: // www. Myweb.com //2019
/xhtml" >

<head>

<title> XHTML Example </ title>

</ head>

<body>

<p style = "color: blue" > My name is John and
I'm a software engineer. I have expertise in Web
Development, C++ Development, Game Development,
Graphic Designing, and Game Development. </ p>

</ body>

</ html>
```

Output:

My name is John and I'm a software engineer. I have expertise in Web Development, C++ Development, Game Development, Graphic Designing, and Game Development.

In the above example attribute of <body> tag is written in lowercase and properly quoted.

HTML Colors

Color Name	Hex Code	Color Name	Hex Code
Aqua	#00ffff	Black	#000000
Blue	#0000ff	Fuchsia	#ff00ff
Green	#008000	Gray	#808080
Lime	#00ff00	Maroon	#800000
Navy	#000080	Olive	#808000
Purple	#800080	Red	#ff0000
Silver	#c0c0c0	Teal	#008080
White	#ffffff	Yellow	#ffff00
Aliceblue	#f0f8ff	Antiquewhite	#ffff00

Aquamarine	#7fffd4	Azure	#f0ffff
Beige	#f5f5dc	Bisque	#ffe4c4
Blanchedalmond	#ffebcd	Blueviolet	#8a2be2
Brown	#a52a2a	Burlywood	#deb887
Cadetblue	#5f9ea0	Cartreuse	#7fff00
Chocolate	#d2691e	Coral	#ff7f50
Cornflowerblue	#6495ed	Cornsilk	#fff8dc
Crimson	#dc143c	Cyan	#00ffff
Darkblue	#00008b	Darkcyan	#008b8b
Darkgoldenrod	#b8860b	Darkgray	#a9a9a9
Darkgreen	#006400	Darkkhaki	#bdb76b
Darkmagenta	#8b008b	Darkolivegreen	#556b2f
Darkorange	#ff8c00	Darkorchid	#9932cc
Darkred	#8c0000	Darksalmon	#e9967a
Darkseagreen	#8fbc8f	Darkslateblue	#483d8b
Darkslategray	#2f4f4f	Darkturquoise	#00ced1

Darkviolet	#9400d3	Deeppink	#ff1493
Deepskyblue	#00bfff	Dimgray	#696969
Dodgerblue	#1e90ff	Firebrick	#b22222
Floralwhite	#fffaf0	Forestgreen	#228b22
Gainsboro	#dcdcdc	Ghostwhite	#f8f8ff
Gold	#ffd700	Goldenrod	#daaa520
Greenyellow	#adff2f	Honeydew	#f0fff0
Hotpink	#ff69b4	Indianred	#cd5c5c
Indigo	#4b0082	Ivory	#fffff0
Lavender	#e6e6fa	Lavenderbluch	#fff0f5
lawngreen	#7cfc00	Lemonchiffon	#fffacd
Lightblue	#add8e6	Lightcoral	#f08080
Lightcyan	#e0ffff	Lightgoldenyellow	#fafad2
Lightgreen	#90cc90	Lightgrey	#d3d3d3
Lightpink	#ffb6c1	Lightseagreen	#20b2aa
Lightskyblue	#87cefa	Lightsteelblue	#b0c4de

Limegreen	#32cd32	Linen	#faf0e6
Mediumblue	#0000cd	Mediumorchid	#ba55d3
Mediumpurple	#9370db	Midnightblue	#191970
Mistyrose	#ffe4b5	Moccasin	#ffe4b5
Oldlace	#fdf5e6	Orange	#ffa500
Orchid	#da70d6	Peachpuff	#ffdab9
Peru	#cd853f	Pink	#ffc0cb
Plum	#dda0dd	Tan	#d3b48c

HTML5

The latest version of the HTML standards and procedures is known as HTML5. HTML5 has new attributes, elements, behaviors, technologies, and the powerful toolkit to develop high definition, fully-responsive, and optimized websites and web applications.

It is a mutual working between WWWC (World Wide Web Construction) and WHATWG (Web Hypertext Application Technology Working Group) to present the content existing on the www in a more structured and responsive way. HTML5 was designed by the Open Source Web Community to enhance the functionalities of the existing web development pattern. Updates and advancements that were made in HTML5 explained below:

- Semantic Elements: Used to describe the content of web page more efficiently such as <header>, <footer>, <section>, and <article>.

- Forms 2.0: HTML5 introduced new form features such as <input> tag to get input from user.

- Local Web Storage: Provides local storage without using plugins. Users can store data on the client-side for the better use of the web.

- Web Sockets: Provides the latest bidirectional technologies for the communication of web applications.

- Provides SSE: HTML5 allows us to launch events from the server-side to web browsers; it is known as SSE (Server-Sent Events).

- Provides two-dimensional surfaces for drawing using JavaScript and CSS properties in Web pages.

- Multimedia: HTML5 provides the facility to embed the multimedia files in your web pages without adding the plugins.

- Geolocation: Allows you to share your physical location with the help of APIs to your web application.

- Optimization: Provides higher processing speed and more significant optimization to run and manage heavy web applications.

- HTML5 also provides the facility to drag & drop the files and objects from one location to another.

Basic Structure for HTML5 Web page is:

```
<! DOCTYPE html>

<html>

<head>

<meta charset = "utf-8">

<title> Title of the page goes here </ title>

</ head>

<body>

<header> Header of the page will be defined here </ header>

<nav> it includes navigation bar of the web page </ nav>

<article>

<section> Body Content will be written here. </ section>

</ article>

<aside> Explaining content will be placed here. </ aside>

<footer> Footer of the page will be defined here. </ footer>

</ body>

</ html>
```

Examples for well-structured HTML5 web pages are:

```
<! DOCTYPE html>
<html>
<head>
<meta charset = "utf-8">
<title> Example for HTML5 </ title>
</ head>
<body>
<header>
<h1> My Website </ h1>
<p> A complete solution to learn all of the
technical programming courses. </ p>
</ header>
<nav>
<ul>
<li> <a href = "/assets /web /main.html"> HTML
</ a> </ li>
<li> <a href = "/assets /web /caa.html"> CSS </
a> </ li>
<li> <a href = "/assets /web /php.html"> PHP </
a> </ li>
<li> <a href = "/assets /web /jav.html">
JavaScript </ a> </ li>
<li> <a href - "/assets /web /p.html"> Python </
a> </ li>
</ ul>
</ nav>
<article>
```

```
<section>

<p> You can learn all of the listed courses from
this platform. </ p>

</ section>

</ article>

<aside>

<p> Other information related to the courses can
be found here. </ p>

</ aside>

<footer>

<p> This is the footer of the web page. </ a> </
p>

</ footer>

</ body>

</ html>
```

Output:

My Website

A complete solution to learn all of the technical programming
cources.

HTML
CSS
PHP
JavaScript
Python

You can learn all of the listed courses from this platform.

Other information related to the courses can be found here.

This is the footer of the web page.

Adding New Elements in HTML5

We can also add new or user-defined elements in HTML5 by using a JavaScript code. Here is the example of adding a new element named <intro>.

```
<! DOCTYPE html>
<html>
<head>
<script> document.createElement("intro") </script>
<style>
intro {
display: block;
background-color: #0c0c0c;
padding: 30px;
font-size: 20px;
}
</ style>
</ head>
<body>
<h1> My Website </ h1>
<intro> Here is the new element added. </ intro>
</ body>
</ html>
```

Output:

My Website

Here is the new element added.

Adding Shiv Elements in HTML5

The HTML5Shiv element is a JavaScript file that is used with the scripts to use the updated feature in HTML5 such as <article>, <nav>, <section>, aside>, and <footer>. Example of using HTML5Shiv element is:

```
<! DOCTYPE html>

<html>

<head>

<meta charset = "UTF-8" >

<! -- [if lt IE 9.0]>

<script src = "https:// www. mywebsite.com
/library /html5shiv /3.7.0 /html5shiv.js"> </
script>

<! [endif]-->

</ head>

<body>

<section>

<h1> My Website </ h1>

<article>

<h2> A complete solution to all programming
courses. </ h2>

<p>Hello! <br /> My name is John and I'm a
Software Engineer. I have expertise in Web
Development, Game Development, and Data Analysis.
</ p>

</ article>
```

```
</ section>
</ body>
</ html>
```

Output:

My Website

A complete solution to all programming courses.

My name is John, and I'm a Software Engineer. I have expertise in Web Development, Game Development, and Data Analysis.

HTML – Quick Quiz

As a quick refresher of all you have learned, take part in this quick quiz – I have provided the answers for you too:

What do the initials, HTML, stand for?

a) Hypertext and Links Markup Language

b) Hypertext Machine Language

c) Hightext Machine Language

d) Hypertext Markup Language

Answer – d)

In HTML5, how do we initialize the document type?

a) <!DOCTYPE HTML

b) <DOCTYPE>

c) </DOCTYPE html>

d) </DOCTYPE HTML>

Answer – a)

Which of the HTML Elements below do we use to make text bold?

    a) <li>

    b) <b>

    c) <i>

    d) <p>

Answer – b)

Which of these HTML elements do we use to create unordered lists?

    a) <em>

    b) <i>

    c) <ul>

    d) <ui>

Answer – c)

Which character indicates a tag has been closed?

    a) /

    b) \

c) .

d) !

Answer – a)

Which font-size does the h1 heading tag use?

a) 2.17 em

b) 1.5 em

c) 2 em

d) 3.5 em

Answer – c)

HTML5 has this number of heading tags:

a) 5

b) 3

c) 6

d) 2

Answer – c)

HTML has this many attributes:

a) 1

b) 2

c) 4

d) 5

Answer – b)

How many attributes are required to add links to elements?

a) ref

b) link

c) newref

d) href

Answer - d)

Why do we need div tags?

a) To add headings

b) To create different sections

c) To create different styles

d) To add titles

Answer – b)

Which tag do we use to make text italic?

a) <i>

b) <italic>

c) <style="italic">

d) <style= "i">

Answer – a)

Which tag is needed for added line breaks?

a) <break>

b)

c) </br>

d) </break>

Answer – c)

Which attribute do we use to open hyperlinks in new tabs?

a) target

b) href

c) ref

d) tab

Answer – a)

How do you add a background color?

a) <body style = "background-color=blue">

b) <body color = "blue">

c) <body style = "background-color: blue">

d) <body bg-color = "blue">

Answer – c)

Which of these is the right code needed to make checkboxes?

b) <checkbox>

c) <input type=" check">

d) >input type=" checkbox>

Answer – d)

Which tag is needed for creating selection lists (drop-down)?

a) <list>

b) <dropdown>

c) <option>

d) <select>

Answer – c)

Which tag is needed for adding headers to HTML5 tables?

a) <h1>

b) <header>

c) <th>

d) <theader>

Answer – c)

Which of these may be used for creating a table in HTML?

a) <table> , <tbody> , <tr>

b) <table> , <tbody> , <trow>

c) <table> , <tb> , <trow>

d) All of these

Answer – a)

HTML Glossary of Terms

Elements and Tags

A tag is a label that defines sections of the markup and separates it into elements. They are a set of angle brackets (< >), containing a keyword. The content is placed between a pair of tags, with the closing one having a prefix of a slash. There are also a few HTML tags that self-close, such as the image tags.

Every tag also has one or more attributes:

The syntax is

<tag attribute='value'>content</tag keyword>

- **Tag** – keywords are head, html, script, body, span, dive, and lots more

- **Attribute** – a property of the specified tag

- **Value** – the value for the tag's attribute

- **Content** – may be a string literal or it could be other HTML tags

Children

A direct descendant of an element or nested inside an element. These are useful when you use pseudo-elements and child selectors (CSS).

In the following example, <li> is a child element, descending from the <ul> element.

<ul id='parent'><li id='child'></ul>

Comments

Like any other programming language, comments are used as a way of explaining sections of the code markup. All HTML comments start with <!--> and finish with --> - see the syntax example below:

<!-- This is an HTML comment! -->

HTML

The fundamental tag for defining html documents; an example of how it is used:

<html> you web page content goes here! </html>

Head

A tag surrounding critical content that the user cannot see but that the browser depends on. The elements in a head tag have page metadata, links to scripts, to stylesheets, and more. The syntax is:

```
<head>
 <title>
 <meta ...>
</head>
```

Title

The title tag is used to inform a browser what it should display as the title at the top of the page and also informs the search engine of the site title. Title tags go within head tags, like this:

<title> HTML Beginners Guide </title>

Titles should be as descriptive as possible without being over the top.

Links

We use link elements to tie documents and relevant resources (not hyperlinks – they appear on web pages). Links will only show up in a document section, not changing any part of the content, just the presentation. They are mostly used or connecting scripts, stylesheets, favicons, even a PDF or RSS feed page format. The attributes used the most are rel and type - here's a syntax example:

<link type='text/css' rel='styles.css' />

Body

A body is a type of container, holing all the content on a page. They follow the <head> tag inside the <html> tag. The syntax is:

```
<html>
 <head> ... </head>
 <body>
 ...
 </body>
</html>
```

Hyperlinks

A hyperlink is created by anchor tags, or it is an anchor that marks a point where another link from the page is held. Commonly, the href attribute is used, directing the link where it needs to go. The syntax is:

<a href='someurl.com'>hyperlinked</a>

Formatting

These are tags to add italics, bold, underline, and other text formatting. They don't get used very often because, unlike <am> and <strong>, they are only for presentation, having no other real meaning. The syntax is:

<b>bold</b>, <i>italicized</i>, and <u>underlined</u>.

Divs

A div is a division of a page, or a container at block-level, for content that doesn't have any meaning semantically. The attributes commonly used are class and id, and the syntax is:

<div id='myID' class='myClass'>...</div>

Headings

The heading tags offer six document heading levels, from <h1> to <h6> - the largest down to the smallest level. These are used for splitting documents into logic, or necessary parts. The syntax is:

<h1> This is the first header! </h1>

Paragraphs

A paragraph tag is the commonest in HTML and is used to show text paragraphs. Often, it will have some other elements inside it, such as <strong>, <a>, <em>, or <img>. The syntax is:

<p> This is a paragraph! </p>

Line Breaks

The line break tag places a line break into a text block. It is often used where a block of text is a single paragraph but requires this type of format, such as an address or a poem. The syntax looks like this:

<p> A piece of text <br/> over two lines </p>

On a web page, you would see:

A piece of text

over two lines

Horizontal Rules

This will create, by default, a black line one pixel in height, running the entire width of the container.

Images

This will embed a specified image in the HTML. The image tag will always have an attribute of src because that lets the browser know where the image can be found. The syntax is·

<img src='agreatimage.jpg'/>

These are self-closing tags and can be used for referencing absolute or local image sources.

Lists

List tags help us to create lists; a <ol> tag is used for ordered lists while <ul> is for lists with no particular order. Both indicate each item in the list with the <li> tag. The syntax is:

```
<ul>
  <li> ... </li>
  <li> ... </li>
</ul>
```

Definitions

These are labels used for defining sections of the HTML markup and for separating them. A set of angle brackets surround a keyword; content is placed between a pair of tags, and the closing bracket has a slash as a prefix.

Semantic Formatting

These are quite similar to other format tags that are no longer used – they have some semantic meaning, and <em> indicates something to be emphasized, while <strong> indicates important things. Both of the elements can help to put across the importance or emphasis level with nesting. The more an element is nested inside itself, the more critical the text inside it is.

References

Altheim, >M., Boumphrey, F. , Guild, H. W., & Dooley, S. (2001). Modularization of XHTML. *W3C Recommendation, April 10.*

Aronson, L. (1995). *HTML 3 manual of style.* Ziff-Davis Publishing Co.

Behr, J., Jung, Y., Keil, J., Drevensek, T., Zoellner, M., Eschler, P., & Fellner, D. (2010, July). A scalable architecture for the HTML5/X3D integration model X3DOM. In *Proceedings of the 15th International Conference on Web 3D Technology* (pp. 185-194). ACM.

Bhullar, B. S., Howard Jr, A. R., & Young, A. (2014). *U.S. Patent No. 8,769,524.* Washington, DC: U.S. Patent and Trademark Office.

Castro, E. (2003). *HTML for the world wide web.* Peachpit Press.

Chen, E. Y., Tan, C. M., Kou, Y., Duan, Q., Wang, Z., Meirelles, G. V., ... & Ma'ayan, A. (2013). Enrichr: interactive and collaborative HTML5 gene list enrichment analysis tool. *BMC bioinformatics, 14*(1), 128.

Chen, H. H., Tsai, S. C., & Tsai, J. H. (2000, July). Mining tables from large scale HTML texts. In *Proceedings of the 18th conference on Computational linguistics-Volume 1* (pp. 166-172). Association for Computational Linguistics.

288

Duckett, J. (2011). *HTML & CSS: design and build websites* (Vol. 15). Indianapolis, IN: Wiley.

Goodman, D. (2002). *Dynamic HTML: The Definitive Reference: A Comprehensive Resource for HTML, CSS, DOM & JavaScript.* " O'Reilly Media, Inc.."

Hickson, I., & Hyatt, D. (2011). Html5. *W3C Working Draft WD-html5-20110525, May.*

Jacobs, S., Gebhardt, M., Kethers, S., & Rzasa, W. (1996). Filling HTML forms simultaneously: CoWeb—architecture, and functionality. *Computer Networks and ISDN Systems, 28*(7-11), 1385-1395. Greer, T. D., Phillips, W. F., & Roden Jr, W. J. (1999). *U.S. Patent No. 6,009,429.* Washington, DC: U.S. Patent and Trademark Office.

Keith, J., & Zeldman, J. (2010). *HTML5 for web designers* (Vol. 1). New York, NY: A Book Apart.

Kopecký, J., Gomadam, K., & Vitvar, T. (2008, December). hrests: An html microformat for describing restful web services. In *2008 IEEE/WIC/ACM International Conference on Web Intelligence and Intelligent Agent Technology* (Vol. 1, pp. 619-625). IEEE.

Ladd, E., & O'Donnell, J. (1998). *Using Html 4, Xml, and Java 1.2.* Que Corp.

Lemay, L. (1998). *Teach yourself web publishing with HTML 4 in a week.* Sams.

Lubbers, P., Albers, B., Salim, F., & Pye, T. (2011). *Pro HTML5 programming* (pp. 107-133). New York, NY, USA:: Apress.

Manovich, L. (2003). New media from Borges to HTML. *The new media reader, 1*, 13-25.

Mittal, Vibhu. "Generating hyperlinks and anchor text in HTML and non-HTML documents." U.S. Patent Application 10/750,180, filed July 7, 2005.

Musciano, C., & Kennedy, B. (1996). *HTML, the definitive Guide*. O'Reilly & Associates.

Pilgrim, M. (2010). *HTML5: up and running: dive into the future of web development.* " O'Reilly Media, Inc.."

Raggett, D., & Specifications, D. T. D. (1996). HTML 3.0.

Raggett, D., Le Hors, A., & Jacobs, I. (1999). HTML 4.01 Specification. *W3C recommendation, 24.*

Robbins, J. N. (2012). *Learning web design: A beginner's guide to HTML, CSS, JavaScript, and web graphics.* " O'Reilly Media, Inc.."

Robson, E., & Freeman, E. (2005). *Head First Html With CSS & XHTML.* " O'Reilly Media, Inc.."

Therrien, B., Süss-Fink, G., Govindaswamy, P., Renfrew, A. K., & Dyson, P. J. (2008). The "Complex-in-a-Complex" Cations [(acac) 2M⊂ Ru6 (p-iPrC6H4Me) 6 (tpt) 2 (dhbq) 3] 6+: A Trojan Horse for Cancer Cells. *Angewandte Chemie International Edition, 47*(20), 3773-3776.

Vaughan-Nichols, S. J. (2010). Will HTML 5 restandardize the web?. *Computer*, *43*(4), 13-15.

Wang, V., Salim, F., & Moskovits, P. (2013). *The definitive guide to HTML5 WebSocket* (Vol. 1). New York: Apress.

World Wide Web Consortium. (1999). HTML 4.01 specification.

Made in the USA
Columbia, SC
11 March 2020

89009349R10163